Dear Pa-Pa...

Merry C

happy n

All my

Liz.

x x x

C000245709

GAMEKEEPING AT HAMERTON

The Changing Times

Gamekeeping at Hamerton

The Changing Times

Albert Spring

The Book Guild Ltd.
Sussex, England

The Book Guild Ltd.
25 High Street,
Lewes, Sussex

First published 1993
© Albert Spring 1993
Reprinted 1994
Set in Baskerville
Typesetting by Raven Typesetters
Ellesmere Port, South Wirral
Printed in Great Britain by
Antony Rowe Ltd.
Chippenham, Wiltshire.

A catalogue record for this book
is available from the British Library

ISBN 0 86332 856 3

CONTENTS

LIST OF CENTRE
SECTION PHOTOGRAPHS

INTRODUCTION

Let me introduce myself.

My mother's maiden name was Edith May Rose, a native of Winwick, and my father was Edward Spring, a native of nearby Molesworth in the old County of Huntingdonshire.

They married in 1913 and their first child was a girl, my only sister, Grace, who still survives.

I was born on the 6th of May, 1916. Our father was in the army, the Northamptonshire Yeomanry, but sadly he was killed in France in 1917. My brother, John, was born shortly afterwards and is still alive.

Our home was a small cottage in a row of eight situated on a hillside half way between Winwick and Hamerton and known as Winwick Hill.

There were so many people living in those eight small cottages in the late 1920s that we could, and did, field our own football and cricket teams.

In 1921 our mother married again so we had a stepfather. His name was Ernest Farrer and at the same time we gained five stepbrothers. His wife had died during the war. While he was serving in France he was blown up and injured so he received a forty per cent disability pension of eight shillings and sixpence per week. Of course, at that time, cigarettes were four pence for ten, bread was tuppence a loaf and money seemed to go so much further when there were two hundred and forty pence to the pound.

Our mother received an allowance from the government because our father had died fighting for his country; but Ernest Farrer got nothing at all for his family.

Yes, it was a lean living but we survived and in my own case it kept me lean and made me mean.

My mother was the kindest person in the world. I'm sorry I cannot think the same about my stepfather.

In 1929 we moved down into the village of Winwick. By this time my sister was living away in service. I can well remember the lady who came to see my mother when my sister left school and engaged her as a servant.

'Grace,' the lady said to my mother, 'seems to be a nice girl. I would like to engage her. I will feed and clothe her and for the first year her wage will be one pound eight shillings for the year and it will be paid half yearly.'

My sister stayed with that lady for a number of years and the family always treated her very well.

When I was fourteen I went to work on a farm. I was an expert catcher of moles and rabbits and I had also reared and tamed fox cubs, young magpies and jays. It was all part of my survival course.

One by one our stepbrothers had left home, in most cases to live and work on a farm.

I never had any problems about employment. In fact I have never been sacked in the whole of my life. Now they call it being made redundant.

By 1935 we were down to our mother, our stepfather, my brother John, myself and our half brother, Victor, who had been born in 1922. I was always kind to him, but only for my mother's sake.

In the mid thirties I was a young man and we all went cycling at weekends in the summer. In winter I was busy catching rabbits.

It was when we were out cycling on Sunday afternoon that we stopped in the street at Clopton about four miles from Winwick. We talked to some friends who were standing in a group on the grass verge. There were two girls with them whom I had not seen before but during the next few weeks a few little enquiries revealed their names. They were sisters, Ivy and Olive Taylor, and their parents lived and worked on a local farm. I had met the girl who, some years later, would become my wife.

Olive and I met and danced together and got to know each other much better. We eventually married a few days after Easter in April 1939 at the Registrar's office but we never had a honeymoon. That was the way it was for working class folk in those days.

In September that year war was declared and I went into the army in February 1940 when I was called up and duly arrived at Spring Hill Barracks in Lincoln.

I didn't mind army life too much and was determined to make the best job I could of whatever I was asked to do. I was young, six feet tall and weighed twelve stone and was full of the joys of life.

I was a good natural shot and a good athlete but I was also a very stubborn person and the army was, I believe, the right life for me. By Christmas 1940 I was a Lance Corporal in the Eleventh Scottish Commando and on my way to Egypt.

I was never static for long and from the Western Desert went to Syria, then back down to Tunisia and up to Italy. I returned to the UK as a full Sergeant in December 1943. As a member of the Tenth Battalion, the Parachute Regiment, I took part in the Battle for the Arnhem Bridge in September 1944 and was finally demobbed in 1946.

Olive and I had a son, Peter, and we eventually, after the war, had three more sons, Arthur, Daniel and Philip. We lived at Winwick all our married life but sadly Olive died in September 1989. It was not a great shock as it had been approaching for some time.

Did we have a happy fifty years? I suppose we were very much like a lot of couples I have known. We knew and enjoyed a lot of contentment and satisfaction with the things we did together and we enjoyed our four sons who are all still alive. Now there are five grandchildren.

FOREWORD

This story is a statement of facts centred mainly around the Hamerton Estate which lies in the north west of what was Huntingdonshire but is now part of Cambridgeshire.

At that time the estate extended to about 2,108 acres and was owned by the Honourable Lady Dorothy Bell and her husband Major Bertram Bell who lived in Ireland at Carrigtwohill, County Cork.

The estate consisted of practically the whole of the parish of Hamerton. At this time Mr Saunders was the vicar and he was also vicar of the neighbouring village of Winwick. The two villages were to share the same vicar for thirty years or so.

This account begins in January 1955 when I was engaged as gamekeeper for the owner of the estate.

The agent for the estate was Mr H. I. Richmond who lived at Chorleton Lodge, Malpas, Cheshire.

Having explained about the absentee Owners and Agent, it is therefore easy to see that whoever was to be their gamekeeper at Hamerton would have to work without on-the-spot supervision, so it was not a job for someone who lacked self confidence or the will to work.

The estate included a small group of farms which together formed a unique community of country people. There was Manor Farm tenanted by Mrs A. B. Steel and her three sons, all of whom were in their teens in 1955. Then there was Grange Farm, the tenant being Mr H. A. Berry. Grove Farm was worked by Mr L. Fortescue and Cottage Farm tenanted by Mr R. Johnson. Salome Wood Farm's tenant was Mr A. Martin. The Rookery Farm tenant was one of the three sons of Mr Carr who lived at Chelveston and last, but not least, Brickyard Farm which, at a later date, was renamed Church Farm. The tenant there was Mr W. H. Berry, the elder son of Mr H. A. Berry at the Grange.

The estate consisted of some 2,048 acres of grazing and ploughed land and about sixty acres of woodland. The Grove Wood was just under forty acres and the other twenty or so were in small to medium size scattered spinneys.

The main crops grown in this area where wheat, barley, beans, potatoes and sugar beet. All the farms carried reasonable numbers of sheep and both beef and milking cattle. This was a very reasonable use of the land which also allowed a fair amount of habitat for wild game including pheasant, partridge, hare and some wildfowl.

The brook, known as Hemmer Stream, winds its way through the estate and on to Alconbury and Alconbury Weston and eventually to Huntingdon and the River Ouse.

In times of flood the people living in the old village often had to live upstairs until the water receded and they could once again move back into their downstairs living quarters.

Life may have seemed slower and quieter back in 1956 but I can assure you that the constant round of a gamekeeper's life was just as hectic as any led by a go-ahead executive. And, of course, there were no plush offices, flashy cars or foreign holidays, just the outdoors in all weathers, being available at all times of the day or night and pitching a constant battle to provide a few good shooting days each season.

It was hard at times, especially when those wielding the cash lacked practical experience as happened on occasion. One just had to plod on and find answers they would accept or try to change their minds.

All in all gamekeeping has been good to me, very good, and in spite of the setbacks, which happen to us all from time to time, I have enjoyed every minute of it. There is nothing to compare with being close to, and in real touch with, nature.

1

January 1955

During this month I had ended my employment as gamekeeper for a private syndicate that was run by Mr T. E. R. Parsons who lived at Glatton near Peterborough. I had been employed by them since April 1948. It was almost totally a partridge shoot and the shooting area included major portions of the parishes of Leighton Bromswold, Old Weston and part of Winwick.

About the middle of the month I received a letter from Mr H. I. Richmond asking me if I would be interested in taking up employment as gamekeeper for the Hamerton Estate. After an exchange of letters we met and talked about it and we agreed that I would take on the job. I had been on the Hamerton Estate, both as a beater and a picker-up with my dogs, on a number of occasions so I knew the ground and was already on speaking terms with the Agent and Major Bell although at this time I had not had the pleasure of meeting Lady Dorothy.

During the 1954 season the keepering had been done by a man living in Hamerton village named Jack Smith. Although he was a very likeable chap he was not really interested in the job and during that last season the total bag of game had been only 140 head of which sixty-three were pheasants, a very poor number for a potentially good shooting estate.

On the 28th of January I officially commenced work and the first job was to make a concerted effort to gain control of the predator population. It was no use considering rearing either pheasants or partridges with a plague of foxes, carrion crows, stoats, weasels and feral cats roaming the area.

To give some idea of what it was like, at Rookery Farm the Carrs were in the habit of lambing about 1,000 ewes and during the 1954 season they lost an estimated 200 lambs to poaching dogs, foxes and carrion crows. The crows pecked the eyes out of the new-born lambs. The Carrs became very good friends to me when this kind of thing was stopped during my first season.

So the predator control got under way. I had always kept terriers that would go to ground to fox. Indeed, at this time I was in the habit of going badger digging with the last of the great terrier men in the area, William Lupton, who at that time lived at Mount Steven Avenue, Peterborough. We called him Tubby.

He was a large man with a well-washed look and his twenty-five stone belied his constant activity. A train driver by profession, he was out with a bunch of his score of terriers every spare moment. He could always be found at the meets of local foxhounds or otterhounds and was there on shoot days at Milton Park with his gun dog, usually a springer spaniel.

Tubby's daughter, June, kept a tame vixen which lived in the house and it would play hide and seek with the local children. However, when Tubby approached, much to his amusement, it hid under the dresser until he was gone. He had never been unkind to it, it just knew that he killed foxes. Regrettably Tubby died of a heart attack in 1963 aged fifty-nine.

Well, I had the terriers for fox but it was no easy matter to find them at home so we had to drive the spinneys and Grove Wood with a gun or two standing quietly at strategic points. The early morning wait for a fox coming home to its kennel was also a very effective method. None of the truly wild creatures seem to be at their peak of alertness in the early hours.

I was once waiting for a fox in the early morning and was lying in a dry grass ditch. The vixen came through the hedge behind me with a leveret in her mouth and she actually put a paw on my foot before she realised I was there. Of course, she got away!

The carrion crows had to be dealt with by gun and trap. Even carrion crows, like pigeon, have their favourite 'sitty' trees and provided that there is sufficient cover to really hide up just before daylight it is almost a certainty that the crows will give you a chance or two inside the first hour of daylight. When they are nesting they are easier to outwit and again they seem much less alert at dawn than at any other time. One thing about carrion crows is that no matter how many one kills there is no fear of exhausting the supply; for every one killed another comes to its funeral.

Stoats and weasels had to be trapped. Fortunately there was no shortage of traps and rat poison. The traps were mainly four-inch gin traps and by the end of February I had set up almost 130 artificial tunnels and I also had a trap in all the dry gateway drains which are the best killing places on any shoot. Unfortunately, it was impossible to reach the ideal density of traps, one to every 200 yards of hedgerow.

Another reason for always maintaining a trapline is that as the keeper walks from trap to trap on his round, he has the opportunity of observing a great amount of predator damage that would otherwise have gone completely unseen. He may notice a few feathers from a blackbird, a thrush or any small song bird. If these are close to the hedge then it is usually the sign of either a stoat or a weasel at work.

On numerous occasions, while on my trap round, I had bitch stoats and weasels dart out of dry land drains and chatter at me. This only happened when they had a litter of young up a drain pipe.

On one occasion a bitch stoat literally flew out of a four-inch dry drain and came within a yard of my feet before darting back. I was carrying a .22 rifle at the time so I lay down in a position where I could cover the drain entrance and see it clearly. Then I squeaked like a mouse and sure enough a half grown dog stoat popped his head and shoulders out of the pipe. I shot him through the head and he fell kicking into the ditch.

There was a flash of brown and white and the bitch stoat had seized the young one I had killed and dragged him back into the drain. During the next ten minutes this happened five more times, but the adult did not show. I proceeded to block the drain entrance with turf and was back in a quarter of an hour with a 2.5 inch gin trap. The turf was removed, the trap carefully set and inserted into the tunnel and the chain tether pegged down. One hour later she was caught and despatched.

Some readers must think what a hard hearted person a keeper must be. Well, I deny this. When you have seen the amount of killing that just one stoat with a family to rear can do, you will then realise why a keeper cannot afford to be sentimental in his work. I regularly found recognisable remains of different birds and animals in and around an earth where a litter of stoats was being reared.

Basically, the object of killing predatory animals and birds is to save the seed eaters from the meat eaters. The seed eaters that are listed as game birds become the prey of the human race. Firstly in the woods and fields in the name of sport and, secondly, in the kitchen in the name of food.

Now before any 'do gooder' blows their top and explodes all over the field, just think of the motor vehicle that is used either by or for the benefit of most people in this country. There you have it, the machine that indiscriminately kills wild life, both predatory and otherwise, to such a degree that, compared to the gamekeeper's toll, it is a miracle the keeper is not issued with a halo.

You may think that up until now I have not written much about the people of Hamerton or about the estate itself. But bear with me and realise that I am firstly explaining the methods that are generally used to produce a shootable surplus of game and other wild life.

Any gamekeeper who carries out selective killing in order that game may survive, if he keeps a record of the predators that he destroys each year, will find that, as hard as he has tried, he has only been successful in taking a very low percentage. Likewise, the sportsman only succeeds in taking a similarly low percentage, about half, of the game crop.

Cats abounded at Hamerton in 1956. Every farmer and every family who worked and lived on the estate had their favourite cat or cats, usually to keep down mice and rats.

At this time, with the exception of the vicar and Mr and Mrs Willis who lived in Chestnut Cottage, every family in the

18

parish made their living off the estate land. Mr Willis worked for an agro-chemical firm selling herbicides and pesticides but after his death in the mid sixties his wife and daughter moved away.

So, if the keeper wished to keep in the good books of the parishioners he obviously could not go around killing off most of their cats. I built wooden cat catchers and these were highly successful. When a cat was caught it was absolutely unharmed and if it was a favourite cat that did not often stray far from its owner's abode then it was returned home and released. If it was a known prowler and killer it was destroyed. In my first year at Hamerton I destroyed 108 adult cats in the woods and fields without creating a single major incident between myself and the farm tenants or workers.

At nesting time the keeper must continue to keep his eyes open for the nests of blackbirds, thrush, linnets and finches. All of these birds, their eggs and nestlings are prey for the stoat and the weasel. The jay and magpie search for and rob these nests too. The holes made by nesting woodpeckers are favourite homes for stoats but I have never found a litter of weasels in such a place. However, if a nest has been robbed of its eggs or young and there aren't any feathers about then it is a safe bet that it could be the work of either a jay, a magpie or a carrion crow.

The blackbird is a great signaller for telling the keeper when either feathered or ground predators are about. If he is making a high pitched 'jink jink' note he is probably looking at an owl, magpie or jay. But if he is making a low note, 'puk puk', then it is usually a stoat, weasel or even a hunting domestic cat.

During my first season at Hamerton, at Grove Wood alone I found and observed forty-one nests of small birds. Of these only one reared its young. All the others were lost to predators, either furred or feathered. The one that was successful had its nest in an old spoutless iron kettle that I'd hung up on a tree and placed half a brick over the hole that would normally be covered by the lid. Thirty years later robins still use the same kettle but it is now on another tree.

When I started my keepering job Fred Goodwin lived at

Hamerton where he had been keeper on the estate for thirty-seven years. He retired in 1952. One day in March he and I walked across Cow Meadow which is part of the glebe land adjacent to the church.

In the middle of the field there was, and still is to this day, a big old Huntingdonshire elm tree. Ten or eleven feet above the ground the first great branches grew out at right angles. Fred pointed to the spot where the lowest branch met the trunk and there, to my surprise, sat a mallard duck on a nest.

'Alb,' said Fred, 'I've been about here for thirty-seven seasons and every year there has been a duck nest on that branch.'

I made a mental note to keep an annual check on the tree and, sure enough, every year since then there has been a duck's nest on that very same branch. Now the old tree is dead from Dutch elm disease so it may not be the home of future generations of mallard much longer.

Before leaving the subject of nesting time I have to say that in spite of the great effort that had been put into vermin control I didn't know of a single game nest that had a successful hatch. However, there must have been some I had not found because I was seeing a few broods of both pheasant and partridge chicks about but the weather had not been very kind so the number per brood was low.

There were a few broods of wild duck along the brook, but the majority of these were late because most of them had lost their first clutch of eggs to predators. They were more successful with their later nests because of the better ground cover at the time.

Whilst walking through Grove Wood in May I had found, entirely by accident, the nest of a nightjar. I had almost stepped on her and had seen her two eggs when she fluttered off in alarm. Later that day I noted that she was back on her nest and I was very careful not to disturb her. I did not visit her again for a week, but when I did the eggs were gone but there was no sign of loose feathers so she may have survived and taken her chicks off to quieter surroundings. Although I have heard nightjars on scores of occasions I have never found a nest before or since.

A bitch otter had reared three young kits in a holt in the base of a hollow willow tree in the Glebe Spinney. I saw them on several occasions before she took them off to teach them to catch frogs, fish and eels in the nearby streams and river.

Tom Joyce senior lived with his wife in a pretty little thatched cottage that stood back from the road opposite to the lane that leads up to the church. He worked for the Carrs at Rookery Farm and during hay time he said to me, 'Keeper, a couple of nights ago I was walking home from work along the brook side and when I got to Black Thorn Spinney (which was the name that Glebe Spinney was known by to most of the old-timers in the village) I saw three fox cubs and you will never guess where they went.'

In a moment it came to me so I said, 'Tom, I would guess that they dived into the water.'

I never saw a person look more surprised than he was! It was several years before I told him why I knew they had dived in.

2

August 1956

August arrived and I was informed that Major Bell and the Agent, Mr Richmond, and his son, Michael, would be on the estate and would like to try for a partridge or two in mid-September.

There was not to be any really organised shooting; in fact, during the whole of this, my first season, Major Bell did not ask his guns to take numbers. He just liked to place his fellow shooters at whatever peg he thought would, during the day, give everyone a fair share of the sport that was to be offered. It worked very well indeed. The master had a very good knowledge of the estate and how pheasant or partridge were likely to fly.

On both days the three gentlemen already mentioned were joined by Mr Geoffrey Butcher. Mr Geoffrey lived with his mother at Manor Lodge Farm, Steeple Gidding, which bordered the estate for over a mile. Mrs Emily Butcher was generous to a fault. She was a great lady and sportswoman in her younger days. She had done a terrific amount of shooting and her knowledge of wild life was of the highest order. She owned a pair of twenty bore guns and would shoot up to six days a week in her prime. Even in her eighties she was not above potting a rabbit from her bedroom window at dawn. This grand old lady died in 1975 aged ninety-three.

Her son, Mr Geoffrey, was a very quietly spoken gentleman, always polite and he had deep knowledge of the ways of the wild. He had shot on many of the grouse moors in Derbyshire, Yorkshire and Lancashire.

I was privileged to accompany Mr Geoffrey on a number of well known grouse moors in the north of England. He was an excellent shot but would only shoot a few birds each day, taking only the highest and most difficult birds. He always had thought to leave a good breeding stock.

When we were on the moors he would say to me:

'Right, Albert. This is your drive. I will load for you.'

Wherever we went everyone seemed to know Geoffrey. It was amazing. We became great friends and indeed we still are to this day. There is only a few months difference in our ages.

We walked up a number of stubbles and a few other fields that had a little cover on them. In 1956 the speed of work on the land was still steady and the burning of surplus straw and stubble had not yet become fashionable. We saw a sprinkling of game wherever we went and everyone seemed happy.

We also discussed the number of shooting days we thought the game crop would stand up to without decimating it. We were talking about entirely wild game as there had not been a game bird reared on the estate or anywhere else nearby.

On the 13th and 14th of September the gentlemen taking part had made a bag of twenty-two partridge and six wild duck. The duck kept getting up off the water in the brook, and once in a while they offered sporting shooting. We also bagged five hares and twenty-two woodpigeon. The weather had been fine and everyone had enjoyed being out in the fields.

At this time there were still a good number of large thorn hedges on the estate and pigeon were continually flying out or over these, often giving very testing shots.

It had been decided that we would try for two consecutive days entirely on the fields and the 12th and 13th of October were chosen. There were to be seven standing guns on each day and I was to engage the number of beaters that I required. When the time came we saw a nice sprinkling of game in each drive. All the gentlemen who were taking part in the firing line were safe and very experienced shots and my beaters were all experienced at this type of job. The bag for the two days was 101 head of which fifty were pheasants.

The gentlemen taking part and doing the shooting were

Major B. Bell, his two nephews, Major A. Bell and Captain J. Bell, Lord Plunket, Mr H. I. Richmond, Mr M. Venning and Mr G. Butcher.

I had engaged several beaters for the shoot. There was Tom Joyce, elder son of Tom who had told me about the cubs that dived into the water. Tom was to beat with me on every shoot day on the estate for the next twenty-five years. Then there was Mervyn, younger brother of Tom, who still lives at Hamerton in the only cottage which still has a thatched roof. He had all the crafts and skills of the old fashioned farmworker including hedge laying and trimming and fervently deplored the modern penchant for hedge removal.

He had been beating for fifty-five years and when he finally retired in 1987 he told me the best times were when he had been working with me. He died in June 1990.

Even if there should be another place after death then I'm afraid we shall not meet again – he lived a far better life than I.

Jim Edwards, who lived at Spaldwick, was another. A haulage contractor in the week, he liked nothing better than to spend his weekends on the estate as beater, picker-up or, occasionally as guest gun.

He loved a good dog, either labrador or retriever, and it was his practice to borrow a trained dog from me and keep it until it died or became so infirm it had to be put down.

Jim was a great friend, a generous man and a practical joker. I invited him for a week up on the grouse moors in the Pennines in August 1979. It was his sixty-fifth birthday and how he enjoyed himself! He worked a spaniel bitch, Princess Christina, which had been given to me, and we had such a wonderful time that he never forgot it. He now lives in retirement at Ellington but still turns out on shoot days.

Charles King was seventy-eight years of age and a great character. With his quick and active mind I think he should have written a book about his life. In his teens he was a pit sawyer and later he travelled the country, fighting in a boxing booth. Although only a small man he seemed to be successful at this though his wages were only a share of the money which was thrown into the ring.

He was landlord of *The Mermaid* at Ellington. There are many stories about Charlie and his pub but the one that really sticks in my mind was told to me by Frank Dickens who was head keeper on the Kimbolton Estate until his retirement in the mid 1970s.

Shortly after the war, Charlie King had some land at Stonely, right on the edge of the Kimbolton Estate. It was harvest time and as Frank looked across the land he could see one of the fields was burnt and blackened with little piles of smoking debris. Amongst this carnage stood Charlie looking as black as if he'd been sweeping a chimney.

Frank discovered the still smoking patches had been sacks of corn and asked Charlie what had happened.

'Well,' said Charlie, 'my son and me finished combining the corn and he took the machine home. Then some stupid ignorant bloody fool lit a fag and dropped the lighted match. The straw flared up and I couldn't put it out.'

'What the hell happened to the idiot who did that?' asked Frank.

'Nothing,' replied Charlie with a twisted grin. 'He's still here. It was me!'

What a character! Charlie was to beat with me for a number of years but we were to lose him in the summer of 1967. I was honoured to be one of the bearers at his funeral.

My uncle, John Payne, was also a beater. He was a native of Hamerton and had been born in one of the old thatched cottages which has now sadly been demolished. Uncle John was one of my regular beaters for many years and it was only his advancing age which put a stop to this activity. A widower living alone for the last twenty-four years of his life, we lost him in 1978 at the age of eighty-four. He had served in the artillery in General Allenby's army in the First World War.

Lastly there was Albert Radwell from Old Weston. He was a bachelor all his life and never, as far as I know, lived outside his native parish. He was one of the regular team until old age stopped him beating after the 1973 season.

The people I have mentioned were all regulars. There was also a number of farm workers I could call upon whenever I required a few extra and they were all good, reliable men. Many of the young sons of the farm tenants also found their way into the beating team from time to time.

In spite of having both young and, shall I say, elderly people on the team, there was never a hint of trouble or argument. Neither did I ever have a cross word with any of the shooting gentlemen.

It was decided that we should try Grove Wood and the spinneys on the 16th and 17th of November. The shooting team was to be the same as before, except that Mr Venning's place was taken by Major Chichester Clark, a gentleman from Ireland. Lord Plunket was not with the team on this occasion so there were six guns each day. The weather was kind and a fair amount of game was well shown.

The bag for the first day was seventy-eight head of which fifty-two were pheasants; on the second day twenty-six out of forty-four birds.

The main reason for the low number of pheasants on the second day was because Major Bell had asked the gentlemen to spare the hen pheasants at the spinneys around the village. We saw three foxes, but shooting at foxes on a shoot day was never permitted at Hamerton.

I was asked to arrange a couple of days to account for a few cock pheasants in January and I chose the 30th and 31st. This was also to give a little entertainment and sport to the tenant farmers. The agent would be there and I asked Mr G. Butcher and his brother, Boyd, and three of the tenants, and this made a nice shooting team of six guns for each day. Again the weather was kind and the bag for the two days was seventy-six with just over half being cock pheasants. This concluded the season's shooting.

The bag for the whole season just about equalled the total for the two previous seasons combined as now there was a little more stock on the ground. I estimated that it would take a full three seasons before we could reach a total of one thousand head per season. Of course I was wrong.

The season's total was 358 head of which 168 had been pheasants, fifty-two partridge, the rest of the bag being hare, woodcock, pigeon and the odd rabbit. It was to be several years before the rabbit population was to build up again after being decimated by that foul disease myxomatosis in 1953–4.

The predators that I had destroyed during that year, not counting the rat poisoning, were three times the number of game shot. Thirty seven weasels were caught in one tunnel trap over a period of six weeks.

Shooting days were important and it was essential to organise them with precision. The marking out of drives was left entirely to me. I usually made a sketch of the shoot plan for that day marking in where the guns were to stand and also the route by which it was hoped they would get to their position. This worked very well indeed and I was never asked to change the plan, although there were times when I had to make changes because of a shift in the wind, a change in the weather or some other unforeseen happening.

When a shoot was being arranged, Major Bell would ask me if there was anyone I would like to ask along for a day's sport. It was only rarely that I took advantage of this kind offer.

After a shoot, which was usually a two-day event, the Major would ask me to ensure that each gentleman who took part had the gift of at least one brace of birds on their departure.

'You will see that all the tenants and any other persons you think fit have game,' the Major would say to me. If there was any over it was sold and the proceeds went to the estate which was a very sound policy.

We never at this stage need professional pickers-up. If a bird was lost either Jim Edwards or Tom Joyce was left behind with their dog to recover it.

At this time I had a beautiful labrador bitch, Flixhill Black Beauty. She was a bit headstrong but a great game finder in any type of cover. I also had a young spaniel bitch named Cherie, also a good game finder and with a lovely temperament.

Then I had a lovely young spaniel bitch named Zipalong Lively. She had been bred by Jack Curtis who lived near Whittlesford. His registered prefix was Whittlemoor and all his spaniels had wonderful temperaments. Jim Edwards borrowed Zipalong and kept her until she died.

27

I also kept terriers. The leader at this time was Spice, a black, tan and white bitch. She went to ground to a fox entirely by accident when she was twenty-six weeks old and she was still going to ground seventeen years later. She was absolutely reliable but a great sports woman. Never in the whole of her life did she kill a fox or badger cub, or even a rabbit.

Another of my terriers was Lady, a rather small but very game bitch, given to me by a great gentleman, Mr Thomas Searle of Whittlesey. I had mated Spice to his very good dog, Sam, but there were no puppies so Mr Searle made me a present of Lady who had been sired by Sam. Bill was bred by me in 1952.

Bill was a much stronger dog. He would kill anything and I can remember when he was my mother's house dog at Vine Cottage. At one time there was a large white sow with eight piglets up in the orchard. When mother went to hang some washing up in the orchard one day Bill, unnoticed, went with her. He sidled round and grabbed one of the piglets by the middle and ran from the orchard, the sow in hot pursuit. As luck unfortunately had it, the back door was open and in went Bill with the piglet, closely followed by the sow. There was such a skirmish and by the time Bill got out into the yard the piglet was dead. What a mess the animals had left in the house!

My mother could have been seriously injured during this episode, perhaps more by the sow than by Bill, but I did come close to having him put down.

One of Bill's better feats occurred when I was following the Fitzwilliam hounds with a couple of terriers in a box in the back of my van. The hounds marked a fox to ground in a nine-inch outfall drain that came off the wartime airfield at Polebrook. I entered Bill, he locked onto his fox and after a while he had drawn its head clear of the drain entrance. Jack Simister, who was huntsman at that time, put his humane killer between the fox's eyes and killed it. The hounds fell on the fox and broke it up and when they had finished Bill jumped into my van still with the fox's mask in his jaws.

When the village children played football on the green in

front of my mother's house they always picked Bill to play as well as he was the best dribbler they had.

We also had trouble with carrion crows. I knew a nest so I stalked to within twenty-five yards of it and saw a crow sitting on a branch above it. I shot it and its mate flew off the nest and landed on the same spot. I quickly dispatched the second crow. That was a game keeper's dream come true.

There were quite a few problems with carrion crows but my friend Eric Goodwin often helped me out with predator control so I knew I could count on him. Youngest son of a local gamekeeper, he did not choose to follow in his father's footsteps but preferred to spend his time with a fishing rod, motor cycle trialling or flying his aeroplane or powered hang-glider.

One evening I got Eric to accompany me to get a carrion crow that was nesting in the long spinney. He was a patient waiter and a hundred per cent successful with his gun and I often made use of his skills.

The plan was for Eric to get in a camouflaged hide in the ditch and I would then walk away across the field. The belief is that crows cannot count so when they saw one of us walk away it would think that both of us had gone and return to their nest.

I told Eric we would try for the pair so I wouldn't come back until I had heard two shots. I had only walked about a quarter of a mile when a shot was fired. I kept walking but as the light was beginning to fade I made my way back to Eric in the spinney, thinking it was a shame only one bird had been killed. But Eric was jubilant. The birds had settled side by side just above the nest and he had dispatched them both with one shot.

'You ought to have fired another shot to let me know,' I said.

'I was so pleased I never thought of doing that,' he replied.

Eric was the only person I know who got two carrion crows with one shot. Eric was Fred Goodwin's son and he still lives at Hamerton.

Another bird I lay in wait for was a sparrow hawk. I had carefully hidden myself in Grove Wood waiting for her to return to her nest. After I had been lying there waiting for an hour and a half I thought I saw a slight movement on the nest. She had been there all the time and so well camouflaged was she that it was not until she turned round that I had spotted her tail feathers.

My first year on the Hamerton Estate had been full of interest for me and was, I hope, worthwhile for my new employer. I had already made inroads into the huge predator population and was at last beginning to see the fruits of my labour. The coming year was going to see a lot more game on the ground, and in the air!

3

It was February. The game-shooting season had ended on the first of the month and I was not happy in my own mind about the previous season.

I had underestimated the capacity to which predators could fill in the areas that had been affected by my efforts.

I was once again busy renovating my last year's tunnel traps and in a number of cases moving them to a different site. Without a doubt the ideal site for a tunnel trap is on one side or other of a gateway and preferably a gateway along one side of a field. Unfortunately most gateways seem to get placed in a corner of the field.

Of course, at this time there was not anyone else anywhere around the estate boundaries who was carrying out any predator control at all. So it had to be a one man band.

By this remark do not think that I had not got a friend because there was Geoffrey Butcher. He was available all the time. There were also Eric Goodwin, Malcolm Houghton from Sawtry. Tom Joyce, Len Fortescue and his son Richard both lived and farmed at Old Weston Grange which they owned. Len was a great sportsman, he often asked me to accompany him when he followed the Bucks Otter Hounds. These hounds were kennelled at Linslade very close to where the Great Train Robbery took place. At this time the Masters were the Uthwatt family and the Huntsman was Lionel Dowse.

We had some wonderful days out with these hounds and I assure you that otter hunting did nothing to cause the great scarcity of otters that was to occur during the next few years.

31

On one occasion when we met at Tinwel on the River Welland we engaged a good dog otter. The hounds marked an old willow tree that overhung the water. Being overconfident, I climbed out onto the outermost part of the overhanging tree and of course part of the tree broke off and I was deposited in the water on my back. This was the highlight of the day. Ever after when I turned up at a meet of the Bucks Otter Hounds I was greeted with a huge smile.

The persons I have mentioned would turn out any evening or Saturday afternoon and on a Sunday. I am sure that all persons mentioned would have missed church to be out with me. Also by this time my own sons had reached the age when they were very capable beaters.

I remember the occasion in April when I had Geoffrey Butcher and Eric Goodwin and myself to stand while Arthur, Danny and Philip drove the wood down to us. By the word drove I mean that they walked well apart through the wood so that any predators would sneak away in front and possibly give the persons who were standing in front the chance of a killing shot.

I had given the boys some pieces of paper and told them that if they saw a pheasant nest to mark the place by leaving a piece of paper close to the nest on a twig. Anyhow when we were all together again I asked the boys if they had seen any nests and Danny said:

'I saw a nest it had nine or ten eggs.'

I said, 'Did you mark it?'

He replied, 'No, but I'll know where it is again because it was not very far from a tree.'

The funny thing is he led me straight to that nest, I marked it and believe me when I checked it a few days later I had a job to locate it.

We had decided that this year I would rear any chicks from eggs that were in nests that were cut out in the hay fields, using broody hens. Of course we had enough nest boxes and coops etc. to rear anything up to five hundred chicks.

Also the Agent was purchasing two hundred English partridge eggs and these I was to incubate under bantams, and

32

when they had started to chip (break through their shells), I was to steal the clutch of wilds nests that I had located in the central area of the estate and place the chipped eggs in the nest. This was the Euston system, but we were not using dummy eggs. I was going to finish up with young partridge with broody bantams.

Of course this was my first venture into this sphere of keepering and so I talked it over with Fred Goodwin. His knowledge in this field was far in advance of my own and so the eggs chipped and the egg changing took place. I found that if I crept up to the partridge on its nest and lay flat on the ground I could ease her off her eggs and place the chipped eggs in the nest quite easily, and the broody partridge would only hiss at me and peck the back of my hand. This stage was easier than I had anticipated. One afternoon I placed twenty-one chipped eggs in a nest with no problem at all.

It was early the following morning that the nest was a terrible sight. There were dead chicks all over the place and, of course, feathers. Here again I was back in my own element. I knew this was not the work of a fox, it was not neat enough. When a fox kills a game bird on its nest there is a little puff of feathers at the nest and usually a little puff of feathers less than a yard away which is where the fox puts the bird down while it clears up the eggs or chicks that the bird was incubating.

I commenced the search and within five minutes I had found both the cock and the hen partridge in a dry ditch, they had both been covered over with dry leaves and twigs. I quickly trapped on both sides of the dead birds and that evening I caught a tortoiseshell cat, a she of course. Now the cat had put those two partridges in the ditch, but on top of the ground, and had covered them over, whereas if a fox leaves a bird that it has killed it also covers it over but before it does this it will excavate a small hole and place the bird in the ground.

The reason the cat had been successful in killing both adult partridges was because when the chicks of the English or common grey partridge are hatching both birds will be in attendance to share the chicks. They are the best parents of all game birds.

33

I was eventually left with some 120 partridge chicks with bantams and seventy pheasant chicks that had been reared from cut out nests, all of which had to go in or beside the Grove Wood. We did not have a rearing ground anywhere else so the pheasants went on the ride in the wood and the partridges on the track alongside the Grove Wood.

At that time I could close and chain the gates at the top and bottom, but unfortunately closing the gates did not stop the tawny owls killing a number of the pheasants or kestrel hawks killing half the young partridge. Oh! how I admire these self-styled naturalists who say this never happens.

The weather was not being very kind either and there were a number of changes taking place on the estate. The old agent, Mr H. I. Richmond, was no longer in charge. He had always been very polite and correct, a typical country gentleman. So much so, that he would never travel on a train unless, in his opinion, he was correctly dressed in a dark coloured suit, his overcoat neatly folded and carried over his left arm along with a tightly rolled umbrella, a briefcase under his right arm; and he always wore a bowler hat.

Bidwells, a large land agent in Cambridge, had taken over and, of course, they increased the rents. Up to this time none of the tenants was paying over £2 per acre per annum. A Mr E. C. Barnard from Bidwells was to administer the estate. I was to carry on as before. Mr Barnard was all right, we got on well together.

Mr H. A. Berry at Grange Farm died. He had been in failing health for some time and his younger son Harry carried on.

It would be wrong to bore everyone with the details of each and every day's shooting during the season. We had the usual two little days in September with three gentlemen each day, the only change being a lady who accompanied Major B. Bell. The lady was Mrs Kingscutt and she resided at Pinkney Court, Malmesbury, Wiltshire. She was a very very intellectual lady and so courteous. She also rode to hounds with the Duke of Beaufort's pack, and was of course always pleased to see a fox.

We held three consecutive days shooting on the fields in October. On the first day there were four gentlemen shooting and on the following two days five. The bag for the three days was 207 head. This was the only occasion that we shot on three consecutive days at Hamerton.

We held two days in November, five guns on one day and six on the next.

There was no more shooting until January when we held a couple of little days for the agent Mr E. C. Barnard, Mr G. Butcher and the tenants. Of course it was for cock pheasants, hares and rabbits; we saw two foxes and several rabbits.

This concluded the season's shooting and there was a distinct improvement. The season's total was pheasants 256, partridge 104, hares 122, duck 8, pigeons 22, woodcock 3, total 515.

We had a new vicar at Hamerton, the Reverend Peter Weir.

We will go directly onto February 1958 and again the trapping round which was not going to be of any great benefit to the wild stock of game. Although in the early spring everything looked very promising, when the month of May came so did the bad weather. It was also cold and wet in June and, if it was possible, it was worse than the previous month.

There is an old saying that a dripping June puts all things in tune but whoever first said that was certainly not thinking about the game that have to rear their young in the wild.

This was the first season that Major Bell and the agent did not walk round the estate to get a partridge or two. In September there were just not any young partridge around.

Of course, the old agent, Mr Richmond, was no longer in charge of the estate and although he kept in touch with me through the post I was never to talk with him again. It was a great pity because he was a real gentleman, so kind and polite, and his knowledge of wildlife was superb. While he was in charge the keeper was one of his top priorities. He even insisted on the very best quality cartridges for the keeper. He would say to me:

'You must have the best cartridges because you must always kill when you shoot vermin.'

Mr Barnard was to shoot in place of Mr Richmond. He was only to be with us for one season, he was to hand over to another gentleman before the next season.

It was decided to hold two shoot days in October which we did on the 30th and 31st. These were entirely on the fields. There were four gentlemen shooting on the 30th and six on the 31st. I only had seven beaters and we did not see a lot of game at all. The total for the last two days was eighty-one head of which fifty were pheasants.

There was no more shooting until 16th and 17th of December when we shot through the Grove Wood and the spinneys. We had six gentlemen on each day and one of these was Captain Anthony Villiers, Major Bell's son-in-law. His wife was the Hon. Dorothy Bell and the Major's daughter was called Rosemary. It was to the children of these two, Valentine, Charles, Hetty and Emma, that the estate would eventually be handed over to and it was their decision to sell.

The two days shooting was, for the season, quite reasonable. The bag was 174 head for the two days of which 142 were pheasants.

Again it was arranged for me to put on two days in January for the tenants and anyone else whom I wished to ask. We chose the 15th and 16th and it was a bad choice. There were a total of seven guns on each day but on the 15th it was so foggy it was hardly safe to shoot.

On the 16th it was terribly cold and frosty and the fog was all frozen on the trees and hedges so that it looked like a fairytale kingdom. In fact Charlie King said there were only two good drives in the two days and they were the two hot lunches; we all believed him. The bag for the two days was fifty-eight head of which nineteen were cock pheasants.

The bag for the season was 313 head of which 211 were pheasants and twenty-five were partridge. All the partridge were old birds.

I had hand-reared eighty pheasants and this was the season that I had hoped that we would make a bag of 1,000 head or more.

A keeper has only one consolation in a year like this and this is it: if he can be successful with his predator control then he can rest assured that he will have as much game about as anyone else in his part of the country.

4

1959

So it was February 1959 and the campaign against the predator was again under way. This was my fourth season and with the exception of the weasel my bag of predators was not varying to any great degree. The weasel population, however, had not recovered from my first season when I trapped 366. Apart from that little killer I was still trapping stoats in the same tunnels and carrion crows still built their nests in the same trees and even the feral cat was far from a rarity.

The Agent now in charge was Mr M. Butterwick from Bidwells. He was a nice enough gentleman but he had not got any great knowledge of the ways of the wild, so fortunately he was only with us for one season.

Another change was at Grange Farm. Mr Harry Berry was to leave us and go to a farm at Sutton against Wansford and a Mr Michael Halford was to take over the tenancy of Grange Farm.

Throughout the whole of the spring and early summer of 1958 we were to have a lot of rain but it was also fairly warm so one thing made up for the other. Apart from a few eggs out of the hay, I had picked up a few early nests from the roadsides and so I hand-reared 150 pheasants. I had built a number of small pens so that apart from feeding the birds and moving the pens and coops they did not take up a lot of my time and I could still maintain my trap line.

The gin trap was banned just about this time and we had been putting the Fenn trap to the test for some little time and it was very good. In 1958 the Fenn trap was priced at 3s.6d. each and today it costs over £4 per trap. What a change!

The new tenant, Mr Halford, was now at Grange Farm and so by the time we got around to the shooting season everything would have settled down once again. There were not any really significant changes as yet in the farming policy on the estate except a slow but sure increase in stubble burning, also the increase in the use of more and more deadly seed dressings and sprays. How anyone could expect to have ample game to shoot whilst at the same time using poisons which affected the seed eating birds was beyond me. All I could do was my best.

This was the time when we began to realise that the magpie was almost a rare bird and that the rooks were a dying race. This was to be traced to the weedkiller dieldrin and eventually lead to the almost complete withdrawal of that dressing from the market.

Four years before this I had recorded 831 rook nests on the estate and now there were just 150 and very shortly there were to be none at all. Those seed dressings did not kill the adult rook but it caused them to produce approximately 70% of infertile eggs, at least that's what the ministry said, and I believe it.

By harvest time it was becoming obvious that this was a far far better season than the previous one. This pleased me very much because I had made a very rash forecast that we would be able to make a bag of one thousand head by the third season and I was by now into my fourth. Of course, keepers should have more sense than to make rash forecasts.

During this year I was asked to accompany Mr Geoffrey Butcher up to Derbyshire when he went to shoot on the grouse moors. I did enjoy these days.

We had a day at Coombes Moss in August, which is a moor close to Chapel-en-le-Frith. It was the first time that I had been on a grouse moor since I was in the army. Then a week later we had a day on a moor called Slippery Stones, situated just above Lady Bower Dams.

The A57 road that runs from Sheffield to Manchester actually runs along the top edge of the first dam. This is wonderful country and I did enjoy being there with Mr

Geoffrey. Everywhere we went there was someone who knew him, not forgetting his mother and brother Boyd. Their ancestral home was at Cutthorpe just outside Chesterfield.

Sometimes we stayed at Chesterfield overnight and sometimes at Castleton, but wherever we stayed no person could wish to be in better company than with any member of that family. I was to make a great number of visits to these moors during the next few years. I was supposed to load for either Mr Geoffrey or Mr Boyd but when I was with Mr Geoffrey he would always say:

'Right, Albert, this is your drive.'

It was fortunate I have always been a very fair shot.

September came and Major Bell visited the estate and on the 7th of that month he, Mr Boyd Butcher and Mr Jack Steel from Manor Farm, had a walk round Grove Farm and Cottage Farm. In the evening they had a duck flight at the moat situated in the cow meadow against the vicarage. The total bag was sixteen partridge, four hares and twelve wild duck on the evening flight. What made me happy was that of the sixteen partridge that had been shot eleven of them were young birds. Remember I had been a keeper on a partridge manor and the number of partridge that we had seen was very cheering indeed. We had also seen a fair number of young pheasants about.

It was decided that the next two days shooting would take place on the 3rd and 4th of November. We had the usual guns except that Mr Butterwick was in place of Mr Barnard. Also there was Mr H. Hillingworth who was, I believe, a stockbroker from London. He was a very fine shot at well-shown pheasants. This made a total of seven guns on the 3rd and on the 4th we were joined by Mr Halford making eight guns for that day.

The weather was fine on the 3rd. We drove the Grove Wood in four drives, then we made up the day by taking out pieces of kale on Manor and Rookery Farms. These pieces of kale had been planted for winter cattle food.

On the 4th we drove out all the spinneys and everyone was happy as we had seen a lot of game. Charlie King was as happy

39

as if he had lost a penny and found a pound. The bag for the two days was a total of 397 head of which 325 were pheasants and 24 were partridge.

We had two more days on the 1st and 2nd of December. There were seven guns for each day. The agent was not with us and his place was taken by Captain David Petherick from Beaconsfield in Buckinghamshire. He was the husband of The Honourable Dorothy and Major Bell's eldest daughter. He was a QC and a very nice gentleman. We were to become great friends and a little later I trained two dogs for him, a yellow labrador named Sam and Julia, a springer spaniel. Mr Hillingworth was not with us on this occasion.

The plan for each day was about the same as it had been for the two days in November. The weather was unkind on the 1st, it was dense fog. On the 2nd we had heavy showers all through the day, but everyone seemed to enjoy themselves and the total bag for the two days was 215 head of which 155 were pheasants.

Once again the shooting for January was left entirely in my hands. We held two days shooting on 14th and 15th. The guns were the two Mr Butchers and any of the tenants who accepted the invitation. Mr J. Fortescue had left Grove Farm and his land was now farmed by Mr John Thornley who lived at Salome Wood Lodge, so he was with us. There were seven guns for each day and the total bag was 128 head of which 61 were cock pheasants. Everyone enjoyed themselves in spite of the cold and snow.

We held a hare shoot at the end of the month entirely for the tenants of their friends. Fifteen people took part and each person carried a shotgun and was expected to act as beater on every other drive. The bag was 180 hares.

This had been a good season. We had hand reared 170 pheasants and had put 541 in the season's bag. Also 72 partridge of which 56 had been young birds, as well as 14 wild duck, 313 hares, 4 woodcock, and 27 various making a total of 971 head. What pleased me most was that we were now getting a good stock of wild game on the estate. It was worth trying hard to get a better result.

Before leaving the 1959 season I would like to say a word or two about the vicar, the Reverend Peter Weir, and his very good wife. They were a very nice couple and the Reverend himself had been in a great many countries. He was wonderful company and always at work around his garden. He was a very cheerful person. He limped when he walked so I gave him a walking stick and ever afterward whenever he required a new stick he would ask me for one, even after he retired and went to live near Saffron Walden.

I was in the habit of cutting walking sticks and thumb sticks. I have never sold one, I always give them away. I still have the same habit.

5

1960

We will go directly on to the 1960 season. The Agent now for the estate was Mr T. G. S. Wilson, from Bidwells of Cambridge, and he was to be with us for a number of years.

There was now a much better stock of wild game on the estate and this gave me more heart to persecute the predators.

There was also another serpent rearing its ugly head now that there was more game about. It was impossible to keep the birds out of sight of the public and the poacher who shot game from a motor car now became a common occurrence. This kind of offence was not easy to stop.

Poaching can be roughly divided into three classes of severity.

The first is the local poacher. He can be anyone who lives in the parish or close to it and he just goes out with his gun and shoots a pheasant for his own dinner, usually early in the morning or late in the evening. These people can be a real nuisance but they will never take enough game to put a keeper out of business.

Whenver this type of poacher is mentioned I always think of the tale told by a certain head keeper I knew. He was awakened after midnight by the sound of gravel clattering against his bedroom window. When he got out of bed and went to the window there was a local man, who he knew to be in the habit of often taking a bird or two for his dinner. He asked the man what he was doing and he replied:

'Keeper, tonight I was in the pub and I overheard several men from the town talking and they intend to raid your pheasants in the early hours of this morning.'

The keeper replied:

'That may be so, but why are you telling me about it when you often take a bird or two yourself?'

The man answered:

'Keeper, I don't mind if these people have yours and your guv'nors share, but dammit, I don't want them to have mine as well!'

That tale portrays the local poacher very well I think.

The second type is the car poacher.

We refer to the car poacher as 'hit and run'. These people drive around the country roads and use either a powerful air rifle or a .22 rifle or a shotgun of usually .410 or sometimes twelve bore calibre. They just knock over any game bird or hare that is close enough to the road to be shot without having to get out of the vehicle. Then the bird or beast is quickly picked up and back into the car and away. These people are a real nuisance but once again will never put a keeper out of business.

I have been successful in catching, or helping to catch, a number of people at this kind of offence and getting them prosecuted. During this year on the Good Friday when all game is out of season I saw two men in a van. One of them shot a pheasant from the van and his companion ran out into the field and picked it up. As soon as he was back in the van they drove off. I kept close to them for about twenty-five miles before they had to stop. I then fetched the police. The van concealed two shotguns, a lot of cartridges, a cock pheasant, three hen pheasants and a partridge. Their apprehension was a job well done and discouraged others of their type.

The third type of poacher is the professional.

The professionals are the worst kind of poacher, always operating at night and only in it for the cash return. Usually working as a little gang of two or three in number, they are dropped off at any time after dark by another member of their gang from a motor vehicle and picked up later on at a pre-arranged time and place. These people need handling with a lot of care for when discovered they invariably offer resistance to arrest. Their most common weapon for killing game is the

43

.410 shotgun equipped with a silencer (sound moderator). If left alone to do their work they will quickly put a keeper out of business.

More about them later on!

The control of predators was again reasonably successful and I was now rearing a couple of hundred pheasants using broody hens to incubate and foster.

As spring gave way to summer it was obvious that we were again to be treated kindly by the weather so as the summer progressed I was optimistic about the season to come and for once I was right.

Major Bell did not visit the estate in September but since there was a great number of wild duck about I wrote to him asking if I could give the tenants a duck flight during that month. He readily agreed.

Therefore, on September 26th we flighted the old brick pit which is about half an acre of water and reeds. Five tenants plus Geoffrey Butcher and Jim Edwards took part. The bag was thirty-six mallard. We could easily have killed a hundred on that evening but we had no wish to do so. All the duck killed were given away either to tenants or people in the village.

Apart from our regular gentlemen taking part in the shooting this season there was a Commander Wyndham Quin. He was a great friend of the Honourable Dorothy Bell and Major Bell. He lived in Ireland, was a good shot and a very nice gentleman. We got on well together.

There was also Mr Wilson, the agent, to take the place of Mr Butterwick. Also in October the Honourable Dorothy Bell came with Major Bell and we were introduced and I was very impressed with her straightforward manner and sincerity. This lady told me that this was the first time she had visited the estate in the last twenty-two years but she did not intend it to be the last.

I will not bore you with the details of each day's shooting that was to take place. I will say only that we held two days in October on the 18th and 19th with eight guns on each day.

Two days in November, the 21st and 22nd, were rained off after only two little drives.

We did not shoot again until January and during this month we held four days. On the 16th and 17th Major Bell and his two nephews attended. There were eight guns each day.

The eight days shooting and the September duck flight had yielded a bag of 1,194 head. Of these 647 were pheasants, of which number 345 were cock pheasants that had been killed in January. There were 112 partridge of which 89 were young birds, a good number, thus indicating that the stock was all right. There were 366 hares, 244 of this total had been accounted for when we held a hare shoot at the end of January for the tenants and their friends. And there were fifteen woodcock. The balance was made up of pigeon and rabbits.

Charles King, our oldest beater, was 82 years of age but he was still going like a two-year-old. What a man!

Tom Joyce senior died during this year, the man who told me about the fox cubs that dived into the water. He was only 72, and one of the last of the older natives of Hamerton. I very much doubt if he ever worked in any other parish during the whole of his life. Two of his sons were to be my friends and be beating with me for the next twenty-six years at Hamerton.

45

6

1961

During the year 1961, mainly in the spring, the fox population was decimated by a disease called fox encephalitis. It affected them very much like canine hepatitis and it really killed them off. There were so many found dead on and around the estate that I began to wonder what I had been doing for the last five years.

This disease was supposed to be caused by the foxes eating pigeon that had been killed by eating seed corn that had been dressed with dieldrin. At this time this was the most commonly used dressing for seed corn during both the autumn and spring seed drilling. Also there was a very large population of pigeon in the country owing mainly to the fact that there was not a market for pigeon at all.

When dieldrin was banned from use on spring-sown seed corn then the pigeons and foxes stopped dying. You must understand that pigeon do not feed to any great extent on autumn-sown grain for the simple reason that at that time of year there is a good supply of alternative feed on the stubble fields.

Once again it was trap and gun to get on terms with the predators. Anyone may think that this is not all necessary. On a number of occasions people have said to me that in the area where they lived there were cats, foxes, stoats, weasels, crows and magpies, you name it they had it, and they still saw the odd pheasant and the occasional covey of partridge. This is true, but what we have to bear in mind is this: if a person wishes to shoot over an area of land, be it woodland, arable or grazing land, for a period of years, then they can only take in one year any shootable surplus. The surplus is the amount of game that is over and above the amount of game that is required to produce the next year's crop. Now, if the land in question abounds with predators there will possibly still be a small amount of game on the land but the pedators will certainly eat the shootable surplus each year. It is as simple as that.

During the spring and summer the weather was fairly kind, a nice lot of sunshine and not a lot of heavy rain. It was obvious that as each day went by we were going to have a happy season.

I found a vixen in a hollow tree with a litter of five cubs, the whole lot were dying from encephalitis. The vixen could not stand up and was frothing at the mouth and rolling about as though in a fit. I took them home with me and phoned a veterinary friend of mine, who was employed by Burroughs Wellcome, a company specialising in veterinary medicines at Cambridge. He came straight away and collected the lot. Unfortunately the vixen died before he arrived.

Although we were appalled by what was happening to a high percentage of the foxes, it was at the same time to help bring about one of the best wild game seasons ever in my time at Hamerton.

The local hunt, like a number of other hunts that operated in arable areas, had to either cut out a number of hunting days or pack up for the season. If my memory serves me correctly, our local hunt packed up for the season on November 26th. A great pity.

There were a lot of broods of wild duck along the brook and also on the few ponds that had not been filled in. As the agriculture was more and more mechanised and intensified at this time about half the ponds had been filled in.

There were broods of wild pheasant and coveys of partridge in every field and it was surprising how well they had fared. We had left the best stock of game birds on the estate that had been left on it for a number of years and this had paid off.

It had been decided that we would hold two partridge shoots and they would be driven days. The days chosen were the 26th and 27th of September. There were six guns on the 26th and seven on the 27th. The weather was fine.

You will understand that these two days were really only small affairs. Each person shooting had just one gun and attended to their own loading. The keeper only had a total of eight people beating and for any flanking that had to be done. We did not even use a tractor and trailer for transport from drive to drive. There was no one with dogs to act as picker up.

How different we were from Mr Joseph Nickerson's organisation when they had broken the record for the greatest number of partridges in one day's shooting. On that occasion each gentleman in the shooting team had three guns and two persons loading for him. There were three teams of beaters and flankers and a small army of people with dogs picking up. They got through twenty-six drives in one day. Their total bag was 2,015 partridge on that one day, that was October 12th, 1952.

But I am writing about our own little days at Hamerton when each drive was arranged so that the keeper and his eight beaters were in the right position for the second drive after they had finished the first one.

We did a total of eight drives on each day. On the first day, the 26th of September, our bag was 106 partridge and 119 on the following day.

Of the total of 225 for the two days, 193 were young birds. When you are dealing with entirely wild partridge it is absolutely essential that the ratio of young to old is recorded at all times. If, in the early part of the season, the ratio of one young to one old bird is counted then only fools would shoot any more partridge during the season.

We know that this kind of counting cannot apply today because many shoots that have partridge in any great numbers have to hand rear them. We were never in my time to do as well again at Hamerton and as an aside we flighted the brick pit at Hamerton in the evening of the 27th of September and bagged thirty-one mallard.

We were to have two more days on the fields in October, there being only five guns on each day and the only difference in the team was that Captain A. Villiers was shooting in place

48

of Major B. Bell's nephew and Commander Wyndham Quin was taking the place of the other nephew.

There were two more days in November with seven guns on the first day and eight on the second, the extra gentleman on the second day was Mr Eric Ablitt. He had purchased Grange Farm in the Parish of Steeple Gidding a year or so previously. This was the first time that we had the pleasure of his company at Hamerton but it was not to be the last.

The one notable item about these two days was that on the first one, on the 16th of November, the bag was 268 head of which 223 were pheasants. This was one of the best days ever at Hamerton.

We held two more days in December and two more in January. The days in January were held mainly for the tenant farmers and then we finished up with a good hare shoot. There were twenty-eight persons taking part. The rule was half stood on each drive and the other half did the beating, then you changed around for the next drive.

You will see that when the fox population was very low through disease the hare population increased tremendously. All keepers are aware that foxes take a very great number of leverets. This is only to be expected because the leveret lives all its life above ground and so is very vulnerable to any predator.

Do not worry for the fox shortage was only to last for the one season and they were to make a very rapid comeback.

So for the 1961 season we had held a total of eleven days shooting on the Hamerton Estate and the total bag for the season was 1,734 head. Of these 756 were pheasants, 339 partridges, 525 hares, 78 wild duck, 7 woodcock, 6 rabbits and 23 pigeon. We were never to get up to this figure again in my time.

There are a few points worth mentioning that at about this time the seed dressing had decimated the pigeons which in turn had decimated the foxes and it had also destroyed the magpie population to such a degree in all the arable areas they were to be a rarity for a good number of years.

Neither the carrion crow nor the stoat and weasel had been affected or the poaching cat. The rabbits were still getting myxomatosis but they were slowly making a comeback because the disease was not killing them in any great numbers like it had done. This was a good thing really from the keeper's point of view because previously, the rabbit, when in reasonable numbers, had always been one of the chief items of food for the fox, stoat and weasel, not forgetting the poaching cat.

When rabbits are plentiful a stoat will average one rabbit a day. One stoat is quite capable of killing 365 a year and I would say that is a very low estimate. Bear in mind that there had only been 170 pheasants reared on the estate during 1961.

7

1962

We will carry straight on to the 1962 season and this was not going to be anything like the previous season in any way. Right from the start the weather was wrong for wild game and, much to my surprise, there were a number of foxes about again. It was exactly as though they had been away on holiday.

We had a very good stock of game, although the system of agriculture was just like a malignant disease: each year it was getting a little bit more intensive. The stubble burning was a more common practice than ever before because, slowly but surely, in the whole of this area the emphasis was for the production of more and more wheat and barley and less and less cattle and sheep.

There was not much use for a lot of straw if there were not a lot of cattle to convert it into food and manure in the winter, so it was put to the torch. Worse was to come.

The only crop that was helping the game in any way at all was a reasonable acreage of potatoes that was still being grown on the estate. On the other hand, it was being sprayed regularly with insecticides. On one occasion I walked round a ten-acre field of potatoes and picked up seventeen dead red-legged partridge. That crop had been sprayed the pevious day with Metasystox, a very poisonous insecticide.

I hand reared 180 young pheasant from eggs that were cut out of the hay or picked up on the roadside.

This season was to give us a total of eight days shooting one of which was a hare shoot at the end of the season. The partridge had done so badly that it was not even considered

51

worth having a walk around the estate in September. That was one thing about Major Bell, he would never dream of arranging any shooting without asking the advice of his gamekeeper.

Therefore we had two days in October with six guns each day, two days in November with seven guns each day. The Honourable Dorothy Bell was also with us. The Honourable Dorothy did not shoot ever.

We had two days in December and two in January. Major Bell attended the two December days and the first one in January. The last day was the hare shoot, mainly for the tenants and their friends. We killed 300 hares on that day.

The season had yielded a total bag of 961 head. Of this total 471 were pheasants, 67 partridge, 335 hares, 28 wild duck, 13 woodcock, 5 rabbits and 42 pigeon.

This had been a poor season because I can assure you that in February 1962 we had a stock on the ground of at least 800 wild hen pheasants and over 300 pairs of partridge. We could have shot a greater number of partridge but we would only have been killing old birds.

8

1963

At the beginning of 1963 we had decided that we would rear just a few more pheasants than in the previous years. We had enough coops and pens to do this. It was not at all difficult to obtain the broody hens required through my friend Jack Engledow at Histon where it was possible to buy all that were needed from Chivers Poultry Farm. I had trained a dog for Mr Stanley Chivers and therefore I was very favoured in that area. Fortunately for me, the dog concerned had turned out very well for what Mr Stanley required.

There was no difficulty in obtaining eggs because there were any number of pheasants nesting on the grass verges and in the hedges by the roadsides. As we did not have a rearing field the only place that I could raise game was on the rides in Grove Wood, therefore when the time came everything was all right.

Before the time for the eggs and broodies came along, the battle against the predators, both furred and feathered, had been, in my opinion, very successful. The gin trap was finished and had been replaced by the Fenn trap which was equally as good for stoats, weasels and rats.

We had commenced catching foxes in snares and by this time I had put in several highly successful artificial earths for foxes.

The weather during the spring was fairly kind to us and everything was going to plan and when egg time came I obtained thirty broody hens from Histon. They were put down on pot eggs and as they settled down to sit the eggs were placed under them. While this was going on I was still maintaining my traps, snares and cat-catching box traps.

In due course the chicks hatched out, there were a number of wild broods about in the fields and the woodlands as well. I was happy and was quietly optimistic, thinking how clever I was.

The broodies produced some 400 chicks which pleased me and everything was fine until the time came when the poults, as they had now become, could no longer be shut in for the night. The tawny owls had a few as did the sparrow hawks and kestrels, but this was nothing really serious; I was not too worried by these losses.

Then things changed. I had half the broodies and poults on the first ride in the wood, the other half on the second ride. One morning at daybreak when I went out on the first ride there were dead poults all over the place. I picked up fifty-seven, there were possibly a few more that had been taken away, it was obviously the work of a fox. On the second ride everything was OK.

I thought: right, the moon is full so I will put a platform up in the handiest oak tree and wait for whatever turns up tonight. I was confident that it would return, so at nightfall I was up on the platform with my gun. I tied a rope around my waist and fastened it securely to a branch in case I dozed off and fell off the platform.

I could see very well, observing several rabbits on the ride, the tawny owls called as did a nightjar making its jarring call. I must have dozed off because I was suddenly awake and sure that I had heard a broody hen cackling. It was not on the ride I was watching but on the other one about two hunded yards away and I was up on the small platform about twenty feet above the ground.

First it was empty the gun and tie a cord onto it and lower it carefully to the ground, then down I went, hand under hand, on the rope that I had climbed up. This all took time.

Cautiously approaching the top ride I found all was quiet. It was half past three in the morning so I fired both barrels of the gun into the air hoping it would put the frighteners on whatever was about. All it did was make a broody hen cackle.

I went home with the moon almost down and the first signs of dawn in the sky. I had some tea and food and went straight back out to the wood. On the top ride when it was fully daylight I picked up forty eight poults. I was rather downhearted and suddenly felt very tired.

During the day I thought about what I should do, too ashamed of what I looked on as my inefficiency to ask even my closest friend to help me, so I decided that I would wait up in the same tower that night but I would hang three lighted stable lanterns on the other ride hoping that it would keep a fox or foxes away and then it might come to where I was waiting.

This I did but it was a terrible job to keep awake and I kept dozing off. Then I was awake, sure that I had heard a hen cackle close by. Then I saw it in the moonlight. It looked exceptionally large and long, it was about thirty yards away. I thought I must not panic, my heart was thumping as loudly as when I once waited with a bren gun in an ambush position. I thought it must hear the safety catch when I pushed it onto fire because by this time it was no more than twenty-five paces away. Slowly I aimed at the thick end and fired.

The creature jumped all over the place making gurgling noises. I stayed on the platform until it lay still, then I lowered the gun and myself to the ground. I put my torch on the creature, the gun in my other hand and I could not believe my eyes. It was a very small vixen. The tawny called again, I looked at my watch, it was quarter past three. I no longer felt tired and went home to breakfast.

The creature when I weighed it scaled just under thirteen pounds, she had reared a litter of cubs and her milk had just about dried up.

Up to writing this I only told my closest friends about it because the fact that this had happened to me was a terrible blow to my pride.

We did not, as far as I know, lose any more of the hand-reared birds that year. We didn't shoot until the 24th and 25th of October, and again on the 27th and 28th of November and the 13th and 14th of January. The January days were mainly for the tenants.

The season's bag was 633 of which exactly 500 were pheasants, 67 partridge, of these only 21 were young birds; the rest of the bag were hares, wild duck and four woodcock.

Captain Anthony Villiers was one of the gentlemen shooting on two of the days. I had not laboured in vain. Captain Villiers was the son-in-law of the Honourable Dorothy and Major B. Bell and it was to his children that the Hamerton Estate was to be made over. At the time that I am writing about none of the children had come of age so the estate was to be put in the hands of two trustees.

Captain David Petherick took part in the shooting on two days during the season. I got along exceptionally well with him and he was a visitor to my house for a great number of years.

The episode with the fox that I have related and which, in my opinion, was created by my over confidence, was never to be repeated during the remainder of my keepering life. It certainly taught me a lesson.

During January, February and March of 1963 we had a lot of snow and frost. It was one of the coldest and longest periods of snow that I was to experience in my whole lifetime. It was hard for both man and beast alike.

9

1964

When preparations were being made for this season there had been a lot of changes. My great friend Geoffrey Butcher was in hospital and was there for a long time. I am pleased to say that he made a good recovery and is still alive today. Major Bell had suffered a stroke, although he again was to make a good recovery and the shooting was to be arranged by his nephew, Major Anthony Bell.

During the early spring and summer the weather was what I can only term average. I carried on with my usual programme of trapping and the killing of both furred and feathered predators. Owing to the uncertainty of what was to happen on the estate I was only allowed to rear some seventy pheasants which were hatched from eggs recovered from nests that had been cut out in the hayfields.

The burning of stubble on the fields after harvest was the worst it had been up to this time. There was no control over how it was done; sometimes it looked as if the whole world was on fire! I would think:

'Why ever did we go to war in 1939? The enemy could not have done a better job of destroying our countryside than our own countrymen were doing.'

Looking at our countryside now I realise that my thinking was exactly right.

The shooting during this season was very chaotic. Often the gentlemen taking part in a day's shooting were entire strangers to me and often the only persons that I knew were Major Anthony Bell and my beaters.

We put in seven days shooting and the only worthwhile days were on the 13th and 14th of November when we bagged a total of 242 head of game of which 223 were pheasants, but on these two days there were eleven guns on each day.

I was allowed to hold a hare shoot at the end of the season for the tenants and their friends and we killed 126 hares. The total bag for the season was 775 head, of which 515 were pheasants.

Mervyn Joyce, circa 1945. The water pump was on
the roadside in front of Mervyn's house

The old Hamerton, viewed from the north-west

Looking north along the main street of Hamerton in
1956

Fred Goodwin with his eldest son, Eric, in the late
1920s

Fred Goodwin with his vermin larder, 1933

The cottage in which Tom Joyce and his family lived
for a great number of years

Hamerton School House
The school was attached to the back of the house,
circa 1940s

The author on a grouse moor at Burnstones,
Cumbria in 1979

A woodcock's nest. One of the few found in the
Grove Wood area in 1982

Moving pheasant poults in 1981. Left to right: Jim
Turner, the author and Malcolm Houghton

The Fitzwilliam foxhounds meet at Hamerton in
1986

Rookery Farm House, the extreme south end of
Hamerton

July 1968. This is how Hamerton looked after 1½
inches of rain in two days

The trap made by the author to catch cats alive and
unharmed

The entry end of the trap when set to catch, circa
1955

10

Again everything was uncertain and so there were no plans as to what would be happening. I went ahead with the spring cleaning of the predator population and hand reared a few pheasants from the eggs I recovered from cut-out nests in the hayfields, a total of ninety-eight.

The weather was kind to us but the system of farming was intensifying all the time and was rapidly becoming the greatest enemy of all types of wildlife.

This was a much easier season for me because there were more persons that I knew participating in the shooting line. We held a total of eight days shooting and I was pleased to see Major B. Bell in the line on two of these days. Although he was looking very frail it was nice to see that grand old gentleman again.

Jack Steel and Mr Halford were regular members of the shooting team this season. Eric Abblitt was a guest on the 18th of December and this was his second invitation to shoot game at Hamerton. He was, and still is, a good shot. For the first time we also had Jeremy Durham Mathews shooting with us, there will be more about this gentleman later. The weather was kind to us on each day. The season's bag was 792 head, of which 667 were pheasant, and the best day had been 155 of which 144 were pheasants.

11

1966

Once again, owing to the uncertainty of what would be happening on the estate, we only reared from cut-out nests and a few picked up eggs. I carried out my usual campaign against the predators.

In the village of Hamerton almost the whole lot of the old thatched cottages had been demolished. This was really a pity because they would have been worth a small fortune today.

It was decided that we would rear a few more pheasants. We purchased a Rupert Rearer during the season and I also reared 120 with broody hens. All this was very successful but the extra birds that we reared could not compensate fully for the losses in the wild state owing to the intensification of agriculture.

Poaching was also becoming more prevalent and the keeper had at all times to be on the alert for the car poachers. I caught several of these and we had a couple of successful prosecutions but they were like foxes, when one was caught another came to the funeral! Also we were losing pheasants at night to the night poachers. It was not being done on a large scale but I knew by the signs that it was happening.

The season came and it was a patchwork affair but we did put in a total of eight days. Once again we had the pleasure of Major B. Bell's company on two of these days but he did look ill, although he maintained his usual cheerful manner.

In both the shooting field and the predator field there were not any out-of-the-ordinary happenings. I was allowed to give the tenants a couple of little days at the end of January.

The total bag for the season was 896 head of which 760 were

pheasants so the 300 plus that had been hand reared had helped us a bit. The weather had been very fair but we could no longer expect any great number of wild birds because of the unnatural farming methods which had become so prevalent.

12

The 1967 season and people

At this time I would like to put you in the picture as to what was taking place on the estate and also a word about my beaters and one or two other items of interest.

The estate had been made over to the four children of Captain Anthony Villers and his wife who, as I have mentioned before, was the daughter of the Honourable Dorothy Bell and Major B. Bell. There had been big changes promised both on the farming side of the estate and on the game side as well. John Thornley, who lived at Salome Lodge, which was not a part of the estate, had been farming Grove Farm which was part of the estate. He was leaving both farms and was going to farm in Australia, so Grove Farm was to be kept in hand to be farmed by the estate. Cottage Farm had become vacant and was to be kept in hand as was Salome Wood Farm.

Do not get confused by me mentioning Salome Lodge and Salome Wood Farm. Salome Wood Farm is part of the Hamerton Estate on the south side and had been farmed by Albert Martin who was retiring through ill health, whereas Salome Lodge is just over our south western border in the parish of Leighton Bromswold. The three farms that were to be kept in hand would total some 600 acres which would in this day and age be a nice sizable holding.

In June Charlie King died at the age of eighty-nine years. We had enjoyed a great number of days together so it was a sorry day for me.

The beaters' lists read as follows at this time:

62

Tom Joyce, his brother Mervyn, Albert Radwell from Old Weston, George Farrer my stepbrother, John Payne my uncle, also Arthur Spring my son, who was keeper on the ground where I used to be partridge keeper twelve years before.

Of course I helped Arthur and he helped me which was fair enough, then we would make up the rest of our team usually from workmen from the farms and very often we had some of the farmers' sons, John Berry, John, Allen and Robert Steel. They all had a good number of days in the beating team.

The vicar at Hamerton was now the Reverend Peter Sutton. He had followed the Reverend Peter Weir who had left us and gone to live at Hinxton near Saffron Walden. He was a much travelled man with a lot of knowledge of people and places.

When he was in residence at the vicarage at Hamerton, on several occasions as I walked past his house on my way to Glebe Spinney he came to the fence and said:

'Keeper, keep your eye open at the Spinney because I saw a cat go across there this morning.'

He was usually right.

The Reverend Peter Sutton was an entirely different person. I well remember that on the 16th of December, 1972, when we had just completed a drive in front of the vicarage he came out waving his arms and was very uncivil just because a pheasant had flown through his dining room window. He said it had landed on his table which had just been laid for lunch and of course the window had been closed at the time! He was so upset about it that I almost asked him if we could have the bird back!

Of course, I got Walter Dodson to repair the damage next day and I paid the bill myself. It was worth it just to see the vicar's face. I still have the receipt. It says:

'For replacing one pane of glass in vicarage window and painting frame etc. £1.50.'

While I am on the subject of people I would like to say a word or two about Walter Dodson. Some sixty years ago when I was a boy and Walter was a young man, he was apprenticed to Mr Gale who at that time lived and had his carpenter's shop at Hamerton. He did all the estate work and had done so for a very long time. When Mr Gale retired and went to live at

Alconbury Weston, Walter kind of inherited the shop and the business. His good wife was also a native of Hamerton. I now wish that I had made a lot more notes when I was talking to Walter. He knew a lot about Hamerton and its people and he was very intelligent but it is too late now. One of his daughters still lives at Hamerton.

At this time when we were in the shooting field I was using a black labrador bitch, Cutthorpe Bet, which I bred out of my bitch Flixhill Black Beauty. She was sired by a field trials champion named Harpersbrook Poacher. This bitch, Bet, had been sold by me at eight weeks of age to my great friend Geoffrey Butcher who registered her as Cutthorpe Bet because his family home was at Cutthorpe, just outside Chesterfield. He had been far too easy with this bitch and at the age of one year she was doing exactly as she wished. So he said:

'You have her back, Albert, and see what you can do with her.'

It took a little time and a lot of patience but Bet became a topline worker in the shooting field.

I was also working a springer spaniel bitch named Cherie. Jim Edwards was working Zipalong Lively, a bitch I had obtained from Whittlesford and she was beautiful. Tom Joyce was still working Whiskey, a springer spaniel dog that I had obtained on the same day as Zipalong. I had sold Whiskey to Tom very cheaply. I paid £18 for Whiskey when he was twelve weeks of age. I kept and trained him until he was ready for the shooting field and then let Tom have him for just the £18 I had paid. You couldn't get cheaper than that! He was a superb dog.

The agent, Mr T. C. S. Wilson who acted for Bidwells the Estate Agents, had a springer spaniel bitch that I had bred and trained, she was an excellent worker and her name was Fly Girl.

Therefore at this time and place, with the odd exception, every dog in our shooting field had been trained by me and most of them bred by me. I am writing this because the names of some of them may come up again.

To return to the estate and how it was faring. The weather was bad practically all through the late spring and summer.

Naturally I carried out my duties of predator control and again reared some 500 pheasants and we commenced the season on the 21st of October having two more days in November. Then came an outbreak of foot and mouth disease in Nottinghamshire, Derbyshire, Lincolnshire, Northamptonshire, Rutland and Cheshire and therefore all shooting was stopped until the 6th of January, 1967. We had to put in a further three days in January. The season's bag was a total of 545 head of which 470 were pheasants.

On the 18th of November Major B. Bell was in the shooting field. I had given him a good man to stand behind him at his request, in his own words: 'To catch me if I fall over when shooting.' I gave him John Payne, my uncle.

Uncle John lived in the row of cottages at Winwick Hill in which I had been born. As soon as he left school he started work at a farm known as Howsons Lodge in the parish of Old Weston. During the First World War he served in the Royal Artillery and was with General Allenby in Palestine during the campaign which eventually defeated the Turkish forces. When he was demobbed he went straight back to Howsons Lodge where he remained for the rest of his working life. Even when he retired in 1959 at the age of sixty-five he still worked on a part-time basis. With his skills as shepherd, stacker, thatcher, hedge trimmer and layer, ditcher, drainer and all round land worker he was almost indispensible.

Major Bell also called him Uncle John as we all did. Sadly the Major was never to shoot at Hamerton again.

13

1968

The grain store was in the process of being erected at Cottage Farm and Peter and Tom Trolove who resided at Great Gidding and farmed there were also farming Grove Cottage and Salome Wood Farms for the estate.

Everything looked promising. They pulled down the old farmhouse at Grove Farm for rubble to use for making a hard roadway from there to Cottage Farm. This house should never have been pulled down as it was in just about as good a state of repair as the house at Cottage or Rookery Farm but, in the name of progress, it had to go.

A lot of promises had been made to the game department for this season but they were not kept so once again we only reared approximately 300 pheasants. Of these some thirty were killed by three dogs which belonged to one of the tenant farmers when they were hunting on their own. This was not imagined or guesswork, they were caught in the act!

This was to be a very poor year for wild game, especially the partridge. We had a lot of rain in June, so much, in fact, that only two partridges were shot during the whole of the season.

We had the pleasure of Master Valentine Villiers in the shooting field on the 18th and 19th of October and I thought he was a nice lad. He was by now a part-owner of the estate.

We held a total of eight shoot days and the total bag was 787 head of which 661 were pheasants with just the brace of partridge. No comment!

It was in February that Mervyn Joyce and myself planted the spinney up on the hill at the end of the field known as

Bakers Barn. It was a success and has given some good pheasant drives during the last ten years or so.

The estate also had trees planted in the place known as the Rough which is one field from Bottom Lodge. They also planted about half an acre beside Rookery Spinney and a couple of hundred trees in what had been the garden and orchard at Bottom Lodge. The trees here were a complete loss because the tenant farmer at that time knocked the wire down by accident and failed to put it up again. Consequently hungry hares and rabbits had a feast clearing up the trees.

The tree planting was part of what had been promised. At least it was something!

14

1969

The early part of the year was the same old story with the battle against predators raging.

There was one, or shall I say two, items of interest during this period.

The first was in April on a very windy Saturday. The gale was blowing from the west and I had, as was our habit, a very early lunch and was back on the estate by half past twelve. I observed a regular flight of pigeon flying up the main dyke at Grove Farm heading towards Old Weston and straight into the wind which kept them very low.

In my vehicle was my gun and cartridge bag and a bill hook. I quickly made a concealed hide in the boundary hedge right in the flight line. Before two o'clock I had fired all the cartridges that I had with me which was about 100. I ran to my van which was about 500 yards away and drove the mile home to collect a carton of 250 cartridges and returned to my hide across which the pigeons were still flighting. They did for another couple of hours but at ten to five the flight stopped.

I commenced my pick up. Cutthorpe Bet was with me and we picked up 268 pigeon and when I counted my empty cartridge cases there were 305. Unlike the people who call themselves pigeon shooters today and leave the area littered with empty cartons, cigarette packets, empty cartridge cases and suchlike, when I left a hide no one could have known if one or fifty shots had been fired from it.

This was the greatest number of pigeon that I was ever to kill in one day.

The other incident was in early May. I had commenced my usual rearing programme and one late afternoon, about ten to five, I was on my way home for tea and to feed my dogs. By the little white bridge on the road between the Grove Wood and the Winwick boundary I observed a stoat run across the road with a young bird of some sort in its mouth. I did not stop as I knew it could only be a bitch stoat feeding young that would do that sort of thing.

I had my tea and fed the dogs then put some Fenn traps in my vehicle and went back to work. Stopping by the bridge I had a look round. It was obvious there were young stoats in a three-hole rabbit set so I proceeded to trap all the approach runs. When I went to look in the morning the bitch stoat was dead in the second trap.

I was very busy at this time so I asked my son, Arthur, to dig the young stoats out. He dug them out and they were only about ten inches deep and there were five of them, thirty-five to forty days old and about five inches long and as thick as a King Edward cigar and perfectly coloured. He got them all out alive.

He then contacted Anthony and Elizabeth Bomford who film wildlife for television including *Survival*. They had at one time lived nearby at Great Gransden but had moved to Gloucestershire. The young stoats were shown on television in a children's film called *Under the Brambles*. Arthur's wife, Linda, found them endearing little creatures and she cried because she couldn't keep them at Hamerton.

Comment: it is enough to tolerate one's friends without harbouring one's enemies!

I reared some 400 pheasants that summer and when they were ready for release in mid July and it was obvious there was something afoot. A lot of rumours were going around but no one informed me of any real change so we carried on as usual.

We held eight shoot days and we had the same gentlemen in the shooting field as the previous year and we all enjoyed the sport. The season's bag was 793 head, of which 675 were pheasants. We had also killed forty partridge of which twenty-one were young birds.

There is another item which I almost forgot which relates to the young stoats. When Arthur dug out the litter he had been very careful to put aside all recognisable items of what the bitch had been feeding herself and her litter on. This is how we sorted it out:

Small leverets nine; small rabbit eleven; wild duck eggs uneaten seven; pheasant eggs uneaten thirteen; partridge eggs uneaten five; and there were enough empty eggshells of game birds to fill a quart pot. There were also the recognisable remains of at least fifty-seven blackbirds and thrushes, mostly young ones. This interested us tremendously as it was a real eye opener.

The 1969 season was a record season for stoats although a lot of hedgerows had disappeared and so a lot of the best trap sites had also gone. I caught a total of 181, of which 156 were males and three of them were white. These white ones were preserved by a taxidermist as they are a rarity in this area and they now belong to my daughter-in-law. In forty years of keepering I have only trapped or shot a total of six albinos.

15

1970

The first thing that happened this year was a very sad event for me as both Fred Goodwin and his wife died. Fred passed away on the 5th of January and his wife a few days later. He had been a good friend and ally to me and so it was a sad loss. We must be thankful that both led full and active lives right up to the end.

During the spring and summer, the weather, as far as game requirements were concerned, was very kind to us. The stock of wild pheasants did very well indeed and so did the 400 that I reared and everything went along very well.

Valentine Villiers came and stayed at Hamerton for a week in the spring and he accompanied me on my trap round each day.

Also this spring a great friend of mine made what was to be his largest bag of pigeon in one day that he was ever to make in his lifetime. His name was John Fox and he was a doctor living in Lanchester, Co. Durham. It had been the custom for Captain John Bell and Dr John Fox to visit the estate, usually in February for two or three days, and shoot pigeons.

I was the man on the spot and I would build hides either on the pigeon flight lines to their feeding grounds or alongside the feeding grounds themselves. During this particular February there was a great number of pigeons feeding on a wheat field that had been down to potatoes the previous year. This was right in the centre of the estate so I built several hides so that if there was a change in the wind direction the shooters could be moved around to what was deemed the best position.

The captain and the doctor arrived on the afternoon of

71

Monday, the 23rd, and it was decided that, provided the weather was kind enough, they would try on the following day. The weather dawned fair with a north west wind and it was fine overhead although it was dull and overcast.

The pair had separate hides and I set up decoy birds for them. They began their shoot about nine in the morning and the pigeon co-operated until half past three. Captain John Bell picked up 113 pigeon whereas Dr Fox had 258 and he had fired 350 shots to do this. I will quote from his letter which I still have:

> '. . . owing to your expertise on siting the hides and making the plan, there was I shooting happily away and in just about six hours, with numerous flasks of tea and coffee, 350 cartridges and 100 cigarettes and, lo and behold, I had bagged 258 pigeon.'

Dr Fox, who smoked heavily, was a tremendous personality and a very fair shot. Regrettably he died several years ago.

During the whole of February and March, to my personal knowledge, a total of 1,750 pigeon were shot on this particular field. The attraction was the potatoes left on the ground from the previous season.

As spring blossomed into summer it was obvious that something unusual was afoot. There were people about on the estate whom I did not know and sometimes they were in the company of people whom I did know. They all had one thing in common: they carried, or had in their cars, papers, plans and maps. By late summer it was confirmed that the estate was to be sold and by September the transaction had been completed.

The purchasers were the Pension Fund of Hambros Bank and the agents acting on their behalf were Cluttons of Great College Street, London SW1.

The shooting was to be kept in hand by the original owners until the first of February, 1971, so it would be shot over by the same people who had been shooting here for the past three or four seasons.

Major Anthony Bell would be organising the shooting side of

the estate until the last day. I was to organise the actual days' shooting with beaters, drives and such like as I had been for the past fifteen seasons.

At this stage I would like to say a little about some of the gentlemen that it had been my privilege to entertain in the shooting field on the Hamerton Estate.

With the estate changing from one owner to another, or in this case from four owners to a committee, it was obvious that a number of our gentlemen would not be shooting with us again in the future.

First of all there was Major Bertram Bell who was, to me and to all others, a gentleman and true sportsman. I never saw him raise his gun to any game bird unless it was flying high and fast. He was a very good shot indeed.

Major Anthony Bell, one of his nephews, was also a very good shot at all times. Another nephew, Captain John Bell, together with his wife, was a most popular person at Hamerton. He was a really good shot and if every gentleman who shot at Hamerton had shot as well as he did then we would not have been able to hold so many shoot days each year. We would have soon run out of birds. It was not unusual for Captain John to shoot all day and pick up a gamebird for every cartridge that he fired.

Mr Hilary Hillingworth, a regular guest in the past and a really first class shot, absolutely excelled on fast, high-flying birds and he made it look so easy.

Captain David Petherick was a son-in-law to Captain B. and the Honourable Dorothy Bell. He was a guest at Hamerton on numerous occasions, was a fair shot, a great sportsman and a very nice person. I had trained two dogs for him, Sam, a yellow labrador and Julia, a springer spaniel and, fortunately for me, they had both turned out very well. Captain David and myself got along very well together at all times and I am grateful that I had his friendship.

I must not forget my great friend Mr Geoffrey Butcher with whom I spent many happy days on the Grouse Moors and on his own farm at Steeple Gidding and, of course, at Hamerton. He was a terribly good shot but so modest about it that one would think it was an accident when he killed an exceptionally high and fast-flying bird. He was also very pleased to see a good dog in the shooting field or my terriers working when he was out with me after some predator or other.

Captain Anthony Villiers was a guest at Hamerton on a number of occasions along with his wife to whom I had been introduced and they were a tremendously nice couple. The captain always seemed to enjoy his days with us but I am certain that he was far more at home in the hunting field!

There were a number of other gentlemen who shot at Hamerton on just one or two occasions and of these I can only say that I hope they enjoyed their time which they spent with us.

During this season I had the pleasure of the company of a good friend of long standing. It was on the 5th of December that Major James Henry Hudson from Yorkshire visited us. He had been secretary to the Fitzwilliam Fox Hounds in the 1950s and we knew each other very well indeed. I am pleased that we had a very good day with a bag of 145 of which 126 were pheasants.

None of these gentlemen were to shoot at Hamerton again during my time. Although they no longer figured in the game book, they were often in my thoughts.

During this season we held nine shoot days. The total bag was 1,168 of which 990 were pheasants. This was nearly 600 above the number which had been reared which goes to show that even at this time good results can be achieved by working at good predator control.

In February 1970 I was finished with the old management of the Hamerton Estate. It was never to be quite the same again.

16

1971

While all the taking over had been going on I was asked if I would consider being employed by whoever the sporting rights were leased to. The new owners intended to keep the sporting in hand and let it on lease to whoever made the best financial offer for it. This arrangement was far from satisfatory for me.

If I was to carry on as keeper then I had to be employed by the owners of the land. A keeper who is employed by the person who just holds a lease on the sporting has very limited powers in dealing with any type of trespasser or poacher on the ground that he is supposed to be keeper over.

It was decided that I was to be employed by the owners of the estate and whoever eventually obtained the sporting rights would be stuck with me along with the sport.

Numerous persons visited me and asked a number of questions and had a look at the game book for the period that I had been keeper and eventually the sporting was let to Mr Jeremy Durham Mathews. This gentleman had been a member of the shooting team on the estate for the past three seasons and so I knew him fairly well, a very sensible person.

He purchased another Rupert Rearer as it was intended that more pheasants were to be reared and I was duty bound to go along with his wishes.

The usual programme of predator control was carried out as intensely as ever in the spring time. It was impossible to maintain a large extended trap line once rearing time came but everything went along all right. The weather during the summer was reasonably kind.

There were very slow changes taking place in the farming scene. Less potatoes were being grown, the emphasis was on more wheat and oilseed rape with tick beans as an alternative crop.

I am convinced that oilseed rape is the worst possible crop that can be grown as far as game birds are concerned, because as soon as the rape comes through the soil there will be every device that one can imagine to keep the pigeons from feeding on it. Game birds are also deterred so that all one will see on the fields are pigeons and the odd hare.

The rape gets really growing during the following summer and the crop will be cut usually in July when game chicks are small and very vulnerable. To make matters worse, more often than not, the cutting is done during the hours of darkness. All this is sporting suicide.

The time came around once more for shooting to commence. There were a lot of new faces on shoot days. Mr Durham Mathews came each day, Mr W. H. Berry was a full gun, Mr Jack Steel and Mr M. Halford both half guns, the rest of the team were an unknown quantity as far as I was concerned.

We got along very well and we completed a total of nine shoot days. The season's bag was 946 head of which 769 were pheasants, so once again we had taken approximately one third more pheasants than we had reared.

There had been a number of one-day-only guests during the season a number of whom came from abroad, among them Herr Hans Konig from Germany and Monsieur de la Selle from France. I could go on for a long time naming all the gentlemen that we entertained during the first of Mr Durham Matthews' seasons but it would not serve any useful purpose.

17

1972

By this time I had completed some seventeen seasons at Hamerton. The predator population was always changing. By this time my annual total of foxes had gone down by one quarter and the magpie and the jay were now rare birds in this area as the seed dressings had reduced their numbers drastically. The carrion crow, on the other hand, was as much trouble as it had always been and there was never to be a shortage of them during the whole of my time on the estate. They seemed immune to everything except a well-aimed shot.

The stoat numbers fluctuated the most. If it was a good spring the population of young rabbits increased and likewise the stoats. The weasel population was on the decline in all arable areas although if we believe the naturalists they will often produce two litters of young in the same season. If this was so they should easily have held their own.

My own opinion is that, like the owl and the hawk families, they suffered through the shortage of field mice and other small animals. These had been almost exterminated by the intensive use of the chemicals in forever trying to boost agriculture yields. When I first commenced life as a gamekeeper the weasel was by far the commonest predatory mammal in any country-side but by this time it was becoming a very rare little animal indeed.

Once again I have strayed from what I was writing about so I must come back to earth. It was intended that I should rear the same number of pheasants as I had the previous year which I did quite successfully.

Up to this time no one had ever been willing to spend any money on equipment. We had two Rupert Rearers, each of which was capable of holding a hundred day-old chicks and it was possible to fill them twice during the same season.

Pens to place these in approximately thirty feet square had been erected by myself using up the rolls of netting and fencing posts that had been in my charge before the estate changed hands. I still had my small pens and coops for rearing with broody hens or bantams. We had been given about one acre of ground at the top of the Grove Wood as a rearing field. It was used during harvest mainly as a stacking ground for straw bales and it was nothing unusual to have a thousand or so stacked up. Wheel ruts over a foot deep proved all the hard work that had gone into moving them.

Every spring I had to fill the ruts with a pick and shovel to get enough level ground for what was needed. Looking back on this now I am sure that at that time I must have been crazy enough to have been committed to Fulbourn (our nearest mental hospital) but no one questioned my sanity and my efforts always seemed to achieve a successful result.

When I am privileged to look around some of my keeper friends' rearing fields and incubator rooms of today I know they have never had it so good. All I ever got was the order to rear a certain number of pheasants and the food to do this with. It was all up to me. We purchased day-old chicks from a game farm in 1972 and they cost about £45 per hundred.

The weather during the spring and summer was far worse for wild game than it had been the previous season.

When the shooting time came around they had decided on eight days. The persons in the shooting field were roughly as before, Mr Jeremy Durham Mathews, the three tenant farmers on the estate, and two more regular guns, Mr I. R. K. Swift and Mr P. Hunt were both very pleasant and above average shots.

The season was very reasonable and the bag was a total of 876 head of which 698 were pheasants. Once again approximately two hundred more than had been reared.

In November I noticed signs that someone had been in the

wood poaching at night. I borrowed a couple of alarm guns from my old friend Jack Engledow and put one in each ride. I waited at the top end of the Grove Wood each night, usually from about ten o'clock until three in the morning. About two in the morning on the last Friday of the month the alarm gun on the farthest ride from me went off.

I was about four hundred yards from the ride. I did not hurry because whoever or whatever had knocked off the alarm could just as easily have been coming towards me as going away from me. I approached quietly and when I reached the spot I found the trip wire on the gun was broken. A hessian sack lay on the drive containing seven warm, freshly-shot pheasants. Whoever it was had been unsure of what was happening when the gun went off, so they had fled, dropping part of their loot.

Surprisingly I had not heard a sound. By the state of the birds they must have been using a silenced .410 shotgun, the poachers' favourite.

18

1973

Everyone seemed fairly well satisfied with the 1972 season. The agents, Cluttons, had allocated a total of eleven and a half acres to go with the sporting right to be used for the express purpose of growing game cover. Unfortunately, the full use of these pieces of ground never came about while Mr Durham Mathews was the sporting tenant.

This has always been a major problem at Hamerton. There are only about sixty acres of woodland on the whole estate and over two thousand acres of arable land. If, at any time, there had been another twenty acres or so of good game cover planted then the whole picture would have changed regarding sporting potential. I could tell some tales about game cover but I have no wish to stir up the mud.

The plan was to be that of the previous year, to raise around five hundred pheasants. The agreements between the agents for the owners and the sporting tenant was eight days shooting with no more than eight guns participating on any one day and no hen pheasants to be killed after the end of December. The agreement was abided by at this time. On some shoot days there would be nine guns but on other days there would often only be seven.

I was always fairly well on the ball so far as the control of predators was concerned and I believed in controlling them, as far as possible, in the spring time. Up to this time there had not been one season in which at least one old vixen had failed to move a litter of cubs into the Grove Wood during the month of May; often a couple of litters moved in.

There are plenty of experts who would prove that these would not do any harm to the game population because they live mainly on field mice and voles. All I can say is that we must have been very short of these creatures.

The largest number of hen pheasants I ever dug up around an earth that held a litter of cubs was thirty-seven. It was in the first week of May when the cubs were some four weeks old. The experts' answer to this would be that they were all sick or injured birds and the fox was carrying out a necessary task in the countryside. The only difference between these thirty-seven birds and the pheasant in winter was that the former didn't have any feathers on their bellies. You work that one out!

The rearing was as usual successful. At no time while I used my Rupert Rearers did my losses exceed eight per cent and I usually kept losses down to around two or three per cent. This was not because I was clever but because I always took what I thought were sensible precautions at all times.

The weather during this season was not very kind and so the wild stock did not thrive well, but in spite of everything there is always the odd hen pheasant that surprises even the keeper by turning up with a reasonable brood of young.

The season commenced once again. We had roughly the same people participating, although I noticed that Mr H. W. Berry only turned up on two days. Much to my surprise the season's bag was 849 head, of which 647 were pheasants, which was only a little below the previous season. We had held the usual eight days, but perhaps the shooting was a bit more accurate!

19

1974

Towards the end of the previous season it had become obvious to me that something was wrong. There had been a sad lack of communication from Mr Durham Mathews, but we went ahead with the same plan to rear about five hundred pheasants to supplement the wild stock. Slowly but surely, like a malignant blight upon the land, the intense system of agriculture was having its effects on the countryside and all that lived in and off it.

There was worse to come. At this time very few combine harvesters were fitted with straw spreaders which ensured an absolutely complete burn-off of corn fields after harvest. Neither had the practice of spraying out hedge bottoms and ditches with weedkiller really started, but more about that later.

Things slowly got underway, the trap round, the search for the carrion crow nests and all the little problems that are the lot of the keeper wherever he practices his trade. The rearing of the five hundred pheasants was successfully carried out.

When the harvest was completed there were the feed places and the water points to be set up for the birds.

During the late spring and early summer the weather had been a little bit below average so there were not a great number of wild chicks to be seen about the estate and this applied to the greater part of East Anglia.

However, a keeper must never be disheartened when the weather appears to go against him because if he has worked hard at predator control he can rest assured that one shoot day he will have as much game on his ground as anyone else and more than most.

Regarding the weather and its effect, this is how I find it works. In a period of ten years there will be one year when everything is as near right as it can possibly be. The sun will shine and all the rainfall will be light and warm, so the gamebirds will do very well.

In the same ten year period there will be one year when everything is wrong. The sun will hardly ever shine and all the rain will be heavy and cold so that nothing will thrive.

In that same period the other eight years will be neither too good nor too bad. The wild game will do just well enough to keep everyone trying for a better year to come.

It rolled round to shoot time again and the usual eight days came and one by one were completed. The gentlemen taking part were almost, to a man, as the previous year and we did quite well, all things considered.

There seemed to be a sad lack of help or consideration for anyone at all and after Christmas I was informed that Mr Durham Mathews was withdrawing from the scene at the end of the season. The sporting was to be relet to whoever made the best offer. Since my services went with the sporting rights, whenever this happened I knew how a slave must have felt in the market place.

At the end of the season, Mr Jeremy Durham Mathews left the scene and I have not seen the gentleman since. I have not got any complaint against him but I believe he was out of his depth as far as running a shoot was concerned.

During this time we had entertained gentlemen from Germany, France, Holland and even a bank manager from Hong Kong!

On the estate the only farmer still growing potatoes was Mr Jack Steel. The rest was down to intensive corn and oilseed rape crops.

20

1975

There had been four different people looking at the game book and around the shoot. Eventually I was told that the sporting was let to Mr D. W. Reeves who, at that time, lived at West Farm, Hinwick in north west Bedfordshire some twenty miles from Hamerton. I already knew this gentleman very well as he was in a shoot at Spaldwick which was keepered by my friend Jim Edwards. He was also in a syndicate shoot at Leighton Bromswold where my son was keeper.

Mr Reeves' keeper at West Farm was George Porter whom I had known before he went there. He was a splendid and very reliable man.

Then there was Mr Jack Cameron who lived at Kimbolton. I had known him a long time and he was one of the last surviving members of a syndicate that I keepered for at Leighton Bromswold in the late 1940s and early 50s. Sadly he died in March 1986 at the age of eighty.

Another member of the shoot was Mr D. W. Smith who owned and worked Poplars Farm at Wymington, also on the borders of Bedfordshire and Northamptonshire. I had not met him previously and was introduced to him by Mr Reeves.

There was also Mr Arthur Brooks, a gentleman who farmed at Leighton Bromswold. I knew this gentleman very well from when I was partridge keeper and he had moved into Staunch Hill Farm around 1953. The farm was part of my beat at that time, and he was a good friend to me and a very good average shot. Regrettably he is no longer with us.

Mr Robin Braid Taylor lived at Swineshead on the border

between Bedfordshire and Cambridgeshire and he was a very good shot at all kinds of game. He and his wife had two daughters and they were a tremendously nice and kind family. I will be forever indebted to them for their kindness to me, especially when we were on the moors in Cumbria.

Major Noel Corry from Steeple Bumstead in Essex was also a very good shot. At this time he was usually accompanied by Eric Wheeler, vicar of the same village and a great character. This gentleman was a most sincere rider to hounds and he owned a big yellow labrador named Toby, affectionately known as Tobe. I had known all three of them before we met at the Hamerton shoot. The Major has written many articles on shooting and antique weapons and he is a much travelled man.

Then there was Mr Peter Carne who lived just outside London. He was a most popular gentleman and tremendously good company. I had met him at the Spaldwick shoot on a number of occasions before he came to Hamerton.

I have deliberately named these gentlemen because they were to be the people who would be shooting regularly at Hamerton for the next six seasons.

The plan was made to rear about 600 pheasants and we also bought in a further 100 ex-pen adult birds so we did not require any more Rupert Rearers. All I did was rear an extra 100 plus with broody hens. It was my friend George Porter who supplied me with all the eggs for this.

At all times communication was good with Mr Cameron and Mr Smith always showing a great interest in the shoot. Mr Smith was to be a great help to the shoot because he did a tremendously good job of getting the pieces of land that went with the sporting planted up with cover for game, mainly in the form of artichokes.

The weather during this spring and summer was kind to us and this pleased me because everyone in the shoot was interested and helpful at all times.

If there were any number of birds after a drive that had not been recovered it had always been my practice to leave either Jim Edwards or Tom Joyce behind to see what they could do about it. At this time Jim was working a springer spaniel bitch named Princess Christina. She was a good bitch who belonged to me. Jim borrowed her, which meant he had her for life.

Tom Joyce at this time was working a young dog named Brandy. I had bred this dog out of Princess Christina by my dog Chaseaway Hector just before I lent her to Jim. Brandy was a good dog for finding game but later in his life he became very quarrelsome with other dogs. Princess Christina was a nice kind little bitch. She had been given to me by a retired keeper friend and I am pleased to say that she gave Jim nine good seasons of loyalty and hard work.

We also had John Drage and his dog, Rover. John was our local policeman and he had commenced joining in with the beating team in 1970. John was instrumental in apprehending more poachers in this area than any other constable in my time, both daytime and nighttime poachers.

We were to hold a total of nine days during this season and they were very enjoyable indeed. These gentlemen were all experienced in the shooting field and knew how to go about the business and when to keep quiet at their stand.

We were well rewarded with a total bag of 1,296 head for the season, of which 884 were pheasants and 145 were partridge. Of the 145, 111 were young birds, all wild bred. Our best day had been the 25th of November with a bag of 219 of which 201 were pheasants. We held a final hare shoot at the end of January in which 183 were killed.

These gentlemen invited all the beaters and myself up to the Green Man at Leighton Bromswold after the last shoot day before Christmas and entertained us with Christmas fare of all sorts which was grand.

Geoffrey Hughes who was acting in Coronation Street and lived at Winwick at this time was with us all day taking photographs; he was tremendously good company and we hope he enjoyed his day.

At this time my old labrador, or rather Geoffrey Butcher's labrador, Cutthorpe Bet, died. We had all enjoyed her work and company for a number of years, but fifteen is a good age for a dog.

I now worked my spaniel Chaseaway Hector. He had been

bred by Mr T. G. S. Wilson out of Fly Girl and his sire was field trial champion Hales Smutt. Hector was a tremendously hard going dog but was always obedient with me, although when my son, Arthur, borrowed him he always made the same remark. He would say:

'Hector is the old man's dog and he only works well for him; in fact, they match each other so well it's a job to know which is the more stubborn.'

I was also working a black labrador bitch named Spey, and she was a good bitch at all times. I had bought her from Tom Ramsey at the Wheatrigg Kennels in 1972. Regrettably Spey never came into season so we never had any puppies from her. She died in 1986, a great friend to me; I hope I was the same to her.

21

1976

The same procedure as usual – persecute the predators, both furred and feathered. The plan was to do as well with the rearing as we had done the previous season and hopefully as well in the shooting field.

In the springtime we had not the slightest idea what was in store for us. During the spring the weather was very patchy indeed, in fact, right up to the first of June. On this day there was half an inch of snow at Hamerton and after that there was hardly a cloud in the sky until early autumn.

The corn in the fields ripened prematurely owing to the drought and all the harvest was finished by the last day of July; the yield was very low.

Jack Steel at Manor Farm had some fifty acres of potatoes but they never reached a size and weight sufficient to make it worthwhile to harvest them. This was the last time any potatoes were grown on the estate.

This weather suited the game birds very well and although everywhere by late autumn was looking bare and barren there was obviously a very fair number about.

At this time my son, Arthur, was no longer looking after the Leighton Bromswold shoot but Jack Cameron still had the sporting right on Salome Wood which is some fifty-seven acres of woodlands on the south west boundary of the estate. It was arranged that Arthur looked after this wood on a part time basis and we shot it along with the Hamerton shoot. Salome made three or four drives, in fact a nice afternoon's shooting. We did not release any pheasants there at all as Hamerton pheasants have always gone to Salome when the weather hardens.

There was one gentleman who had joined the shooting team this season, Sir Kenneth Butt who farmed in Lincolnshire; a very pleasant gentleman as they all were.

We had a minor poaching incident on the seventh of September. I observed a Volkswagen parked in the field adjoining the Grove Wood. It was unlocked and the keys were in the ignition. I put them in my pocket. It was about three o'clock in the afternoon and after waiting some time two American servicemen came out of the wood. They were carrying a powerful air rifle and five nearly adult dead pheasants. When I told them who I was they did not seem very impressed. When I asked them for their names and addresses they refused to tell me. I asked them to hand over the gun and game and they refused to do that also. In fact they were downright uncooperative. Fortunately Allen Steel came along the road on a tractor and I asked him to go and ask his father to phone the police.

The police arrived some fifteen minutes later and it transpired that besides the offences of trespass in pursuit of game, killing game out of season, killing game without being in possession of a current game licence, they did not have any insurance for the car. This cost them a lot of money, whereas if they had co-operated with me in the first place I would have gone up to their base and complained to their authorities. They would have got off with a stern lecture. I had done this on several previous occasions so I cannot understand the stupidity of these two men.

There was a much more serious incident in November. I had known for a fact that night poachers had been in the Grove Wood during the previous season on at least two occasions, so I decided that I would watch out there every night, at least through November. This meant that I had to get a little sleep whenever I could. It is always interesting to be out late in the countryside.

On the night of the 16th of November I was alone and had been in the top end of the wood for some four hours. I had

89

neither heard nor seen anything unusual and at about three o'clock I decided to take a ride down to the Spinneys to see if everything was all right there; it was. I decided to go home and snatch three hours sleep. On my way I had to pass the bottom end of the Grove Wood and some one hundred and fifty yards before I reached it there in the middle of the road crouched a cock pheasant. I almost ran over it.

I knew that there was someone in the wood, so I drove on until I could no longer be seen and parked the van in the field, got my torch and walked quickly back and stood quietly beside the wood. After a few minutes I heard two people coming down the side of the wood.

Thoughts raced through my head. If I let them get too close and they decided to take a pot shot at me, the closer they are the more it will hurt. So when they were about twenty-five yards away I shone my torch on them and shouted as though to a dog:

'Go and get them, boy.'

They both turned to run but one slipped and fell down. By the time he was on his feet I was up to him and then I fell over something. I thought it was a man but it was only his jacket and there were twenty-five pheasants in the lining. He had shed it to get away. I got going and again fell over something, the other person's jacket. This had allowed them to get a clear lead on me and after all, I was sixty years of age.

I returned to the jackets, both identical, with the linings stuffed with pheasants. My problem was to get the evidence out of the way in case they decided I was on my own and returned to make a fight of it. The jackets were hidden and I ran to my vehicle and drove to Hamerton and woke up Arthur who phoned the police. When they arrived they put checkpoints in all the roads but they were too late. From the time of my contact with the poachers to the time the police arrived was forty minutes.

It was a further twenty minutes before a police tracker dog arrived. I accompanied the sergeant with his dog for over a mile and a half but lost the trail on the Old Weston/Winwick road. We returned to the Grove Wood and emptied the jackets and found twenty-five birds in each lining and that was that. I now know who it was but it is too late, even to give them their jackets back.

During the rest of the season I watched at the Grove Wood every night but nothing untoward happened.

The weather and the predator control served us very well this season so we held a total of nine days shooting. We picked up a total of 1,537 head of game of which 1,164 were pheasants, 223 of which had been shot at Salome Wood on three separate afternoons during the season, but unfortunately we did not get there again. We had killed 247 partridge during the season of which 198 were young birds; they were nearly all red legs.

The pheasants I had reclaimed from the poachers are counted in the bag.

Everyone was very pleased with that season, especially myself. A gamekeeper is an entertainer and he enjoys the season that enables him to give exceptionally good entertainment.

22

There is one thing I would like to make very clear – during the 1976 season everything had gone in our favour, the weather, the predator control, and the fine weather on shoot days. We just had not been able to go wrong so all the gentlemen had been as pleased as we were. George Drage, who was a life-long friend and a fairly regular beater, had made the remark that he was sure I must have been doing something like going to church to get a season like 1976.

What am I getting at? The 1977 season was to be a below average season. The weather was wrong all the way through. This was to be the first season we had failed to recover the number of pheasants that had been released although the gentlemen appeared to be as pleased as they had been the previous year. They were all countrymen and they knew what was required to make a bumper season possible.

There is no point in writing too much about this season at all. The predator control had been as successful as it had been the previous season. The rearing had been as successful as well, but there were hardly any wild chicks to be seen of either pheasant or partridge. Even young duck could be seen floating paddles uppermost in the brook. There was nothing that anyone could do about this kind of thing.

We held a total of nine days shooting during the season but the last day was a hare shoot when we killed 148 hares. There was a bitterly cold wind and it sleeted all day long. We all echoed Charlie King earlier saying: 'The only good drive was the lunch'. There had been plenty of hot soup laid on which we really enjoyed.

This year had to be a disaster for it was the year that great character Charlie King passed away on the longest day, the peak of the English partridge hatching. There are not any English partridge in this area any more, more's the pity, only the red-legged variety.

We got through the season. The total was 1,000 head including the hare shoot. We had killed 555 pheasants but I had released 600. We had 134 partridge of which 51 were young birds, but we had left a good stock on the land in spite of it being a poor year. No hens were shot after the end of December.

There was one item of interest towards the end of January bringing us into the next season.

I was going to Sawtry to see Tom Joyce. My wife was with me and it was just before eight o'clock in the evening, a moonlit night with patchy fog in the low places. We had passed the estate boundary by some two hundred yards when I spotted a vehicle on the side of the road against some trees. A man ran over and got into it. I could see he was carrying what appeared to be a gun, so I drew in front of his vehicle, got out and shone a torch on his number plate. He bawled out in a very rude manner:

'What the hell do you want?'

I replied most politely that I only wanted his number for future reference and then I drove off.

After a while I noticed a vehicle trying to pass so I pulled into the side of the road to let it go. As soon as it was in front it pulled up and a person jumped out. I sensed trouble so I told my wife to stay in the car whatever happened.

I opened my door but before I could get out our friend had grabbed me by the tie and gave me a couple of right handers, then I was out of the car. Now, you would-be fighting poachers take note – don't grab a person's tie if that person was a qualified instructor in the SAS.

I was twenty years older than the other person but he was on his back in the road with his jacket pulled over his head in two seconds flat. I made him crawl to his vehicle, his companion had already jumped into it.

23

During the early part of this year we were fortunate in the fact that a life-long friend who lived at Great Gidding had retired from work. He was seventy years of age but very fit and fed up with not having enough to do as he had been a hard worker all his life. He and I had been friends for over fifty years; we had caught rabbits together by practically all known methods so it was natural for him to come along with me on some of my rounds. His name was James Turner; we will refer to him as Jimmy from now on so that we do not confuse him with our other old friend, Jim Edwards.

Most days I picked him up in the morning and we did the trap round together. Jimmy had lived in the country and knew the ways of the wildlife very well indeed. If he came back from visiting traps and said a carrion crow had taken a nest of eggs or a vixen had taken a game bird off its nest or he had found a partly eaten game bird covered over and he thought it was a wild cat, then I went with him to investigate. I usually found that he had read the signs about right.

Jimmy was not like me about these things. If and when he found the signs of game birds, rabbit or hare being taken he was very annoyed about it and seemed to think it was a very personal affront that predators should do that kind of thing. However, I had realised for a long time that as long as you had a reasonable stock of game then you would have a reasonable stock of predators that would take their share without asking permission. After all, the only certain way of doing away with bank robbers is to do away with banks!

In spite of a very successful campaign against predators and a successful rearing time we were still not to be favoured by the weather.

The only time the weather was dry and warm was when straw burning time came around and it was about this time that the evil practice reached its peak in this area.

Public opinion was beginning to have a bigger effect on the way this was done and there were strong demands from the public for more control. You may think that the fact that I call it an evil practice is a rather drastic description. Well, in all this writing I have only written facts and believe me, I once picked up twenty-two hares that had been burned to death on an eighteen acre field that had been burned off by dragging a burning diesel-soaked sack around the field.

I have seen hares on fire running into a fresh field and start that burning. I have seen game birds so stupefied by the smoke that they have flown and settled right in the fire and burned. Once a pair of English partridge continually ran in and out of the burning stubble making the same agitated call as they do when a stoat or a poaching cat is after their young. I am pretty sure that these birds had a late brood of chicks in the fire area.

The time came around to commence the shooting again. The team of guns was very much the same, although there was often a guest who had been invited to take the place for the day of one of the regular guns.

On a couple of occasions Mr D. W. Reeves had invited a gentleman, a Mr S. Whitbread from Bedfordshire. I believe he was Mr Reeves' brother-in-law. When this gentleman was a guest he usually brought his gamekeeper, Tom Norris, with him. He was one of the family of Norrises that had been gamekeepers for a great number of years for the Duke of Bedford at Woburn Park.

Tom was one of my adversaries in the days when we used to attend the annual clay pigeon shoot for gamekeepers held at Madingley, organised by Gallyons, the gunmakers at Cambridge, so naturally we had a lot to talk about.

A total of eight shoot days was decided on. They were very pleasant too. The total number of pheasants that came to hand was some twenty below what had been reared, once again the wild birds had not done very well. I was not downhearted because we still had a reasonable stock on the ground. The season's bag read like this: total bag 834 head, of which 580 were pheasants and 53 partridge, eleven of these being young birds and all were red legs.

We held a hare shoot on the 11th of February. Although the land was very wet, we killed 111 hares which brought the total bag for the season to 945 head.

On the 13th of January Jack Steel of Manor Farm passed away. I was terribly sorry about this as we had enjoyed some good days shooting together, also some great times with the terriers after foxes.

In August, at the kind invitation of Mr Reeves, Jim Edwards and myself spent a week up in Cumbria on the grouse moor. It was superb and we really enjoyed ourselves. There were a great number of grouse and we were looked after very well indeed by all the people at the shooting lodge where we made some very good friends indeed: Mary Armstrong, cook at the lodge, her husband, Sid, the keeper, Johnnie Parkinson, and his wife, Janet. I have been back there again since that time and everyone was just as kind. Wonderful Days!

24

1979

One very noticeable thing right from the beginning of 1979 was that once again there was a big build up of the stoat population. Of course, we were already aware that their populations vary greatly from season to season for no apparent reason. We used the same tunnels for trapping year after year and approximately the same number of traps and then suddenly, bingo! There seem to be stoats everywhere. This did not create any real problem and we quickly set about getting them under control.

We planned to rear chicks again as we had the previous four seasons which was around 600 pheasants. This was arranged and successfully undertaken.

Jimmy was with me practically every day which was a great help. Mr and Mrs Cameron visited the rearing field about once a week and we had the pleasure of seeing Mr D. W. Smith from Wymington very often, usually on a Sunday, and he always brought his cine camera with him. He had made some splendid films of shoot days and other things of interest in a keeper's life. I said splendid films – well at least I thought they were. I suppose I was bound to say that as I was in them!

Also we often saw Mark Brown, who had become a regular member of the beating team who usually accompanied Mr Peter Carne. We got over the problem of two Marks by making Mark Smith Mark One and Mark Brown was Mark Two. He was an ex-Irish Guardsman and we got along very well indeed.

Mark Brown was a very keen rabbit catcher and if myself or

one of the beaters caught a rabbit as we often did, Mark Brown would say:

'I bet it has got MB on it.'

Of course, this meant that it would be his at the end of the day. It usually was.

We held a total of eight days shooting during the season. Usually there were nine gentlemen taking part on each day and as usual Mervyn and Tom Joyce still took a very active part in the beating team.

This, once again, was a very successful season and throughout every shooting day the atmosphere was one of good comradeship and friendship.

In the eight days we made a total bag of 994 head, of which 751 were pheasants, 107 partridge, 38 hares, 46 wild duck and 14 woodcock, the total being made up with odds and ends like rabbit and pigeon. Of the 107 partridge that had been killed 69 were young birds.

We must bear in mind that we had released about six hundred pheasants and no one had fired at a hen pheasant after Christmas so I thought it was a very successful season. On top of that, the company had been good and I do not know of much else that a person could wish for.

25

1980

There was a funny smell in the air. By that I mean there were a lot of rumours going around the tenants regarding the sporting rights on the estate. They felt that as the rents for sporting rights were so high then they should also reap some of the benefit.

Another problem was Dutch elm disease which had spread over about two thirds of the Grove Wood. It had been advised that these trees should be felled as soon as possible while the wood was still in a condition good enough to bring a cash return so this was set in motion. Felling two thirds of the Grove Wood and making a total clearance in the area would mean the temporary destruction of just over one third of the woodland on the estate.

During the spring and early summer we carried on with the same successful rearing programme that we had developed over the past few seasons. It was essential to carry out the usual battle against both furred and feathered predators and I was helped by Jimmy.

The weather was average to good during the spring and summer and we reared another six hundred pheasants successfully.

The public were still up in arms about the stubble burning after harvest; even those in town protested at the smuts which would invade their homes for two or three weeks during the burning period. They realised their country heritage was in danger and protested, and rightly so about the agricultural policy which allowed their countryside to be turned into an ash heap each autumn.

I had seen so many acts of stupidity while straw and stubble was being burned that at times it made me feel sick, and believe me, I have a strong stomach.

Now, back to what was happening on the estate. It was quite obvious to me that something was afoot, but it didn't worry me a great deal because in May the following year I would be sixty-five and then, in that old expression, I would be able to 'take it or leave it'.

Slowly but surely the year rolled by until it was once more time to take up our places in the shooting field and the atmosphere was as pleasant as it always was. I had already been informed that Mr D. W. Reeves would no longer be the tenant of the sporting rights on the estate after the end of January 1981 which did not come as a shock to me, it just made me sad to think that he was leaving. Whilst he had been with us the estate was a very happy place to be involved with and we were still good friends.

We held the planned eight shoot days with nine gentlemen on each day. As far as I was concerned it was a very successful season and I believe everyone else agreed with me.

The season's bag was 1,161 head and we held a hare shoot in mid January which added 167 head to the total. The bag read like this: 796 pheasants, 55 partridge, 243 hares, 11 woodcock, 23 wild duck and of course there were the usual rabbit and pigeon that went to make up the total bag. Of the partridge killed only nineteen had been young birds so they had not done very well that season.

The syndicate run by Mr D. W. Reeves finished with the Hamerton Estate on the 1st of February, which was a great pity.

26

From the 1st of February the sporting rights on the estate were taken over by the three tenants, Mr W. H. Berry, Mr M. J. Halford and the three brothers John, Allen and Robert Steel, who since their father's death, were farming at Manor Farm. This was to be known as the BHS Syndicate which it still is some seven years later.

Things had become a little bit complicated as far as I was concerned. As I was not due for retirement until May the syndicate was stuck with me until then. I had drawn up a list of permanent equipment like traps and chicken coops and pheasant pens and these had been taken over from Mr Reeves.

As soon as the ground was dry enough to support heavy equipment, the elm trees in the Grove Wood were to be felled and cleared and the timber sold to Mr M. A. Henderson of Norsdale Sawmill situated near Grantham in Lincolnshire. I had been asked by the agents, Cluttons, to be their representative on the spot at this end.

The area to be cleared covered about twenty-six acres and work was begun on the 21st of June and was completed at the end of September. During this two and a half month period only a few minor problems arose. I had to destroy a number of wasps' nests and several colonies of bees which had made homes in a few of the trees which were to be felled. There were also six hornets' nests to be dealt with and as these insects can be dangerous when angered great caution was necessary. One chap, Peter Thompson, was stung on the forehead and it knocked him out as if he had been poleaxed.

I put one of the hornets' nests into a plastic bucket and covered it well and took it home with me. After it was dark and they were quiet I removed the lid and placed a sheet of glass over the top. I fed these hornets on both brown and white sugar for a couple of weeks so that all the children and most of the adults in the village could have a look at them walking upside down on the glass. The queen hornet was over two and a half inches in length.

After two weeks I took the hornets, complete with their unbroken nest, and placed them in a hollow tree in the Glebe field at Hamerton and they survived for the rest of the year. You may wonder why I was not stung. Well, I had kept bees for nearly forty years so had a little bit of knowledge about how to treat their wild cousins, the main thing being 'the gentle touch'.

There was another incident concerning hornets during the summer. I had a gigantic nest in my cabin in the Grove Wood which they built up from half an orange to about the size of half a football and I have photographs to prove it. I used that cabin every day and was never molested by them.

Now you may think I was a fool to go in there but never at any time did I enter that cabin without first knocking and calling out:

'It's all right, it's only me.'

On occasion I would be in there in my shirt sleeves with several hundred on the wing but I was never once stung.

My son, Arthur, was with me one evening and I told him about the hornets in my cabin. I said that if he wanted to go and look at them then he must tap on the door and announce himself.

He laughed and said I was 'bloody crazy, man'. He opened the door without knocking and a hornet hit him between the eyes and he fell to the ground as if he'd been shot. It was ten minutes before he came round and I couldn't help saying:

'Who's crazy now?'

My old friend Jim Turner wouldn't go near them and he, too, thought I was crazy.

If I had owned anything of great value at the time, that is where I would have kept it, in the cabin with the hornets. They were great at keeping people at bay.

After the felling and tidying up was completed at the Grove Wood, the people from Norsdale Sawmill erected rabbit-proof wire netting around the area that had been cleared and during the winter of 1981–2 it was replanted with a mixture of hardwoods and conifers including oak, ash, poplar, spruce and larch, a good mixture.

Returning to the sporting on the estate, the time came in May for my official retirement. The pension fund, through the agents, Cluttons, treated me very well and indeed also gave myself and my wife a small pension towards which we had contributed not one penny piece. This we greatly appreciated; after all, there was no law to say that they should, and I had only been in their employ for ten years.

The BHS team now had the sporting tenancy and planned to release about 800 head of pheasants and by the month of May this had to be well under way.

A number of secondhand Rupert Rearers were purchased and since there is not a lot that can go wrong with them they were more than adequate. I had been asked to catch about seventy-five hen pheasants and ten cock birds for egg production which was fine but I was expected to keep these birds in the same pens to be used for rearing the chicks which was asking for trouble. The eggs we obtained were hatched by Nigel Roberts at his game farm at Folksworth. We managed, of course. Most keepers are good at managing and the losses were not excessive but it cost enough in medication against coccidiosis and gapes to rear the same number again if it had been done on clean ground.

As I say, we managed, and as it was coming round to shoot day once more we had come to an arrangement that kept me employed on a part time basis.

It was planned to hold a total of nine shoot days with ten guns taking part on each day. I was, as before, expected to select the beaters and organise their day. Tom Joyce had been suffering from arthritis or some form of rheumatism for a number of years and said that he couldn't manage a full day any more so he would not be with us. Since he had practically

103

always been there on shoot days during my twenty-six years at Hamerton he was very much missed by me.

Mr W. H. Berry, Mr M. J. Halford, Mr J. Steel and Mr E. Chattell were full guns and Mr J. Bowyer, Mr C. Covine, Mr D. Rampley, Mr K. Roe, Mr D. Saywell, Mr P. Jackson, Mr J. Otter and Mr E. Harper were half guns.

Most of these gentlemen were known to me and everything went very well although as the season progessed I realized that most of the people in the syndicate were using the shoot for the purpose of inviting their friends along. I did not mind this but it doesn't make for a very happy day if the keeper is not aware of who is actually taking part in the shooting team.

We got through the season successfully with a bag of 960, of which 729 were pheasants, 86 partridge, 79 hares, 2 woodcock and 34 wild duck. I had fed the duck on the brick pit and we had flighted them on three different occasions. There was also the odd rabbit and a pigeon or two to make up the bag. Regarding the woodock in this area, some years there are a good number about and other years hardly one is seen. Twenty nine of the partridge were young birds.

27

It was planned that this season the shoot would have an incubator so that we could hatch our own chicks. An old Westernette incubator was purchased but due to lack of forward planning it was one disaster after another. Again I had to catch around seventy hen pheasants and again they were housed in the pens that would later be required for rearing and to act as release pens a few weeks later. Of course, it could not go on like that for very long.

I managed to supply the eggs for the incubator but I did not have anything to do with the running of it as it was clear from the start that it was going to be trouble. When it was full, with around one thousand eggs, it cooked the lot! This meant that I had to go running to one of my long standing friends for chicks. Fortunately the weather had been reasonably kind during the nesting season and this helped considerably.

Eventually the time to take to the shooting field arrived once again and the team of participating guns were the same as for the previous year and eight shooting days had been planned.

The bag for the season was good with a total of 1,039 head, of which 826 were pheasants, 49 partridge, 41 hares, 8 woodcock, and 97 duck we had flighted from the brickyard pit, on four occasions successfully and twice not so well.

We had released around eight hundred pheasant poults but that foolish policy of shooting just a few hen birds after Christmas was creeping in, which is sporting suicide. Of the partridge only eighteen were young birds.

It was no use worrying about what was happening on the

estate or in the shooting field. At this time land values, as far as agricultural land was concerned, were on the downward trend so houses and anything else that was on offer were being sold off. It was the beginning of the break-up of the Hamerton Estate as we had known it in the past, a sad state of affairs. Also I had thought that once the farm tenants had taken over the sporting on the estate there would be any amount of game cover but sadly this was not so, it was in as short a supply as ever it had been. By this time chemical farming had reached its peak which meant almost total destruction to any type of wild game.

Jim Turner often said to me:

'Well, mate, you saw the time when you reared less than a hundred birds and saw over a thousand shot in a season. Before long you will see a thousand reared and less than a hundred shot.'

During the whole of this season we had the pleasure of the company of Wing Commander Frank Harrison who lived at Barham. He attended each shoot day along with his yellow labrador to do the picking up. A very good job he and his dog made of it!

28

At the commencement of 1983 it was planned to release about one thousand pheasants. This meant that around eight hundred would be purchased as six to seven week old poults. It was desirable that these birds should be delivered to us about the end of July so that with a bit of luck a fair amount of the harvest and stubble burning would be completed while these birds were still down in the release pens. Everything was arranged and all went well.

Jim Turner and myself had worked away at the predators. You must understand that on a shoot like we had, surrounded by unkeepered ground, it was essential that the carrion crows, stoats, weasels, poaching cats and foxes had to be kept down to a reasonable number otherwise the shoot would be in trouble and trouble was what we could do without.

The weather was very kind throughout the nesting period which helped a lot. At least it meant that there were a few wild pheasant and partridge chicks about but the only places these could survive, of course, were in the patches of woodland on the estate.

The gentlemen in the shooting team were as for the previous two years although I noticed that more often than not they asked a friend to a day's shoot. This did not bother me, I was too old a hand at this game to let it worry me. We held a couple of very successful flights at the wild duck and seventy were killed.

We held eight days shooting during the season and we had what I thought was a very good bag of 1,180. Of this total 916 were pheasants, 80 partridge, 45 hares, 5 woodcock and the 70 wild duck. Of the partridge 35 were young birds.

All the experts tell me that partridge will stand a reasonable amount of shooting without harming the stock, providing that the ratio is not less than one young to one old.

During this season, once again Wing Commander Frank Harrison and his dog favoured us with their company and made an excellent job of picking up. Of course, this gentleman had great knowledge of the shooting field scene and he was always tremendously good company. It was very regrettable that due mainly to falling health, the Wing Commander could not continue his and his dog's activities with us after this season and we missed both of them.

29

1984

During the spring and summer of this year the weather was not anything that could be termed wonderful but it was not too bad. It could have been a very fair season if, in the first place, we had had anything like a good stock of partridge, but that was just wishful thinking.

The shooting team was the same as for the three previous seasons. The plan was to release the same number of pheasants as the previous year and this was done successfully at the due time.

The shooting season went well and we ended up with a total bag of 1,099 of which 899 were pheasants, 54 partridge, 108 hares, 21 woodstock and 23 wild duck. Twenty-four of the partridge were young birds.

For some reason there were a lot of woodcock in the area this season and it was nice to see them about.

We had only flighted the duck on one evening during the season. There were plenty of duck about and as I have said before no one wished to shoot them just for the sake of shooting them, but it was nice to have a duck to eat. As an ex very keen wildfowler, I have never sold a wild duck on my own behalf at any time.

There were a lot of hares about this season which meant that the year had not been unkind. After the harvest was completed and the burning carried out there was a big public outcry against the practice yet again, and quite rightly so. This practice held second place to chemical farming as far as damage to our flora and fauna were concerned.

Each year after harvest there was a public outcry about burning and the NFU* would be putting all sorts of excuses and writing about controls to lessen the damage but the time was coming when people were beginning to realise it was just a big bluff on their part.

The reader will see by the pheasant numbers why I said the releasing during the summer was successful. One thousand released and 899 put in the bag was a good figure and I have known shoots do far worse.

* NFU – National Farmers Union

30

1985

The modern system of arable farming had by this time just about reached its peak and it was impossible to imagine anything more intense in the way of sprays and machinery. On the whole of the estate there was not one field that grew a leaf of wild white clover, it was impossible to find flowers like cowslips, daisies or buttercups except in the shelter of the woodlands where the sprays had not drifted over the land.

As soon as the corn was gathered by the combine harvesters the hedge trimming machine would travel around the hedge-rows that were still allowed to remain on the land. Of course, this was also the time just before the blackberries started to ripen and so there were a couple of thousand acres on which it was almost impossible to pick enough blackberries to make one small pie. My comrade Jim Turner always, at this time of year, carried an empty coffee jar in his pocket and if he found blackberries in one of the pieces of woodland he would pick them and take them home in his jar. The funny thing is that he always said that he never ate any of them either in a pie or in jam, he said there were too many flies peeing and pooing on them for him to eat them, his words, not mine.

I could remember the time when my mother often picked forty pounds of blackberries in a day and a gentleman called Bumper Nicholson came round twice a week and collected them paying two pence per pound at the start of the season but this would soon go down to a penny ha'penny, this being in the days of 240 pence to the pound. Bumper Nicholson died not long ago.

111

The plan for the season was to release about one thousand pheasant poults as we had done the previous year. Of these eight hundred were purchased as poults and Jimmy and myself reared a couple of hundred or so to make up the total required. Of course, as usual we carried out our battle against the predators in the spring and we caught up enough hen pheasants to produce the eggs that we required for the broody bantams to hatch out. We were still using the same small pens I had made thirty years ago.

Everything went according to plan, both trapping and rearing. One thing I must mention is mink. Each summer we were regularly catching a number of these creatures, usually around five or six. We never saw them about at all and they left little evidence of their habitation on the estate. The only time we saw them was when they were caught in one of the tunnel traps.

When it was for the time for shooting to commence there were a couple of alterations in the shooting team. Two half guns, Mr J. Otter and Mr E. Harper had withdrawn and were replaced by two others who had a half gun in the syndicate.

The weather had not been unkind although it had not been all that good. Sadly the partridge stock was severely depleted so we knew there would be very few.

So the season commenced and we held the usual eight days plus flighting the wild duck on the brick pits on four occasions resulting in the bag of fifty-eight birds.

The total bag for the season was 962 with 776 pheasant, 49 partridge, 62 hares, 8 woodcock and the 58 wild duck. We had seen very few woodcock about during the season and of the partridge shot only twelve were young birds.

The amount of game cover was still pitiful. My comrade, Jimmy, summed it up when he said that game cover was the only crop on the Hamerton Estate that fails. Short sightedness leading to over zealous clearance of unsightly scrub and no long term plans for the continuance of shooting were the main reasons for this.

Poaching was reaching serious proportions, particularly of hares. It was carried out quite openly with people coming from as far afield as Kent and Staffordshire. Sometimes there would be as many as twenty in one party and they were quite blatant about their activities; they would take notice of no one except the police. Often when I saw them I would say:

'Right, if I was you I would move on quick as you can as I've phoned for the law.'

Sometimes this worked, sometimes it didn't.

We also had a young lad as trainee keeper under the government youth training scheme. His name was Paul Presland and he came from Abbotsley some fifteen miles away. He was a likeable chap but this was not the place for a trainee keeper. He wanted to know all about incubators and intensive rearing methods which are how it's all done today; he didn't want to know about the make do and mend that was the practice at Hamerton. He stayed for his full period of one year and I do hope that he enjoyed this time with us. Unfortunately, I do not know where life has taken him since.

31

During the nesting season the weather was very patchy all the time. It was not very warm and sunny for more than a few days together, nor was it spectacularly wet; it was basically grey when the sky was clouded for days on end.

Once again Jimmy and myself waged war on the predators and we patched up the pheasant pens once again. When the time came we reared our usual two hundred plus pheasant chicks under broody bantams. At the end of July we received eight hundred poults which did very well and they were eventually released into the Grove Wood and the spinneys. We always released about five hundred poults at the Grove Wood and the balance were distributed amongst the other spinneys on the estate. This spacing out of the birds gave them plenty of living space and they did very well.

This season we held an extra days shooting, the ninth day being a hare shoot. The guns taking part were the same as the previous year. Most of the 136 hares killed were on land farmed by Mr M. Halford. That particular day made the season's total look better and it also put a little bit of extra cash into the bank.

This was how the season's total was made up: 844 pheasants, 68 partridge of which 22 were young birds, 182 hares, 14 woodcock and 51 wild duck which we had flighted on three separate evenings. Seventy-two hen pheasants were shot on the two days of shooting held in January 1987. This is a very poor policy and can only lead to disaster on a shoot like the Hamerton Estate.

Up to the last five or six seasons we had already killed more pheasants than we had released but even so the recovery rate was about 80%. This was mainly because by leaving a fair number of hen pheasants on the ground there were always a few that reared their own chicks.

In the early part of the 1986 there was a hen pheasant that always came up to the same feed place in the Grove Wood. She was very lame and I said to Jimmy that I'd have to kill her but I never did. After we stopped feeding the pheasants we didn't see much of her until early June when she turned up again in the same area, still limping, but with four lovely chicks in tow. Every day I carried a good handful of chick crumbs in a bag in my pocket and fed her and her chicks and they survived well all summer.

This was the last season that Mervyn Joyce came beating. He said it was time to pack it up as he had been beating on the estate for over fifty years.

I bet he won't forget the morning in 1959 when I had him out on stopping the pheasants from leaving the Grove Wood which we intended to shoot that day. It was bitterly cold with hoarfrost everywhere and we were out before daybreak. I had taken half a pint of rum mixed with hot water and sugar as a warm-me-up tonic. Mervyn had a couple of good pulls at the bottle and when I went to where he was supposed to be later on I couldn't find him. Eventually I found him asleep in a ditch amid the sparkling frost. He was none the worse for this, thanks to the rum which had put him there in the first place.

32

This was to be the season that brought about the greatest changes to the Hamerton Estate in living memory. For several years the owners had been selling off any vacant cottages or farmhouses on the estate. During 1987 they also sold approximately half the land as well. By doing this it meant that basically the estate no longer existed. When the selling had been completed, the Steel brothers owned Manor Farm, a total of some seven hundred acres. Mr W. Berry and his son John now owned Church Farm and part of the Rookery farmland whilst Rookery Farmhouse and the Rookery Spinney had been sold to a Mr and Mrs Miles.

The Manor Farm house had been sold to another party as a private residence as had Church Farm farmhouse. Also the keeper's cottage and Chestnut Cottage as well as ninety acres of what had been Rookery farmland. This had been sold to a Mr Brooks so it had really developed into a big carve-up as far as the estate was concerned.

Please do not get the idea that I was against any of this happening because all I am doing is relating the facts about what was happening. I could not really care less as there were now very few real natives of the estate to care about it either.

Mervyn and his wife Kath still lived in the one surviving cottage in the one time centre of the village.

The thousands of young trees in the Grove Wood were being sadly neglected with a large number of them badly overgrown by briars. If these trees reach maturity it will be through the efforts of Jim Turner and myself because we have kept the

116

rabbits and hares under strict control when they got over, under or through the wire.

To give you some idea of what this entails I will relate one incident. In the summer of 1984 a man came with a tractor and a jungle buster and had several days trying to clear between the rows of young trees. Every time he turned he caught the wire netting with his machinery and the result was a great number of holes through which hares and rabbits entered. We repaired the holes and caught eleven rabbits and four hares in one five acre area alone. The jungle buster was so badly damaged by repeatedly hitting old tree stumps that only about one quarter of the area was ever completed. So much for modern methods and machinery!

Now back to the sporting side of the one time Hamerton Estate. The whole of the parish was still shot over by exactly the same people but we were no longer allowed into Rookery Spinney except for the purpose of recovering any dead or wounded game birds from it. This was a pity because the Rookery had always given us at least a couple of interesting drives each season.

Right from the start of this season the weather was bad and as the year progressed the weather got worse. I would think that 1987 was one of the years when rainfall in the area was the heaviest that has ever been recorded.

There was no hope for either the partridge or the pheasant in the wild and the incidence of gapes in hand reared birds was very high indeed. Of course, as usual with us, we had taken all reasonable precautions both against the weather and the predators so we were not caught out when eight hundred pheasant poults arrived at the end of July. All we really wished for were just a few days of reasonable weather. You will understand that the poults that were being purchased were reared entirely in heated buildings which means they never feather up as well as birds reared in the open. Someone must have known about our wish because we got almost a week of reasonable weather and this meant that our losses were no greater than in any other season. The weather did cause a certain amount of inconvenience because the grass tracks got so wet that we had to walk and carry food for the birds for a good part of the time but as Jimmy remarked: 'Well, at least we don't have to carry any water!' Jimmy always looks on the bright side.

We had to cancel our first day's shooting that had been planned. It would have been on the 12th of October entirely on the fields. The harvest had been so prolonged by the bad weather that the farmers were still very busy trying to catch up with autumn sowing. Anyhow, there was next to nothing on the fields. This was not brought about entirely by the very bad weather; it was partly brought about by the simple fact that there was not at any time any consideration given to the game on the land. This was only considered on shoot days. There was not a good stock of game on the land so we only held seven days shooting during the season. The persons taking part in the shooting team were the same as in the previous season.

The total for the season was 823 head of which 762 were pheasants, 8 partridge, 20 hares and 7 woodcock. The rest of the bag was made up of rabbits and pigeon, and fifty-one hen pheasants which had been shot in January.

It was my intention to end this writing at the end of the 1987 season and I think that is the most appropriate time to do so.

This is the time to say thank you to all of the ladies who participated in making the shoot days a success either by accompanying their menfolk in the shooting team or in the picking up with their numerous dogs. Also thanks to the gentlemen who took their stands in the shooting field through-out the thirty-odd seasons. They were many and varied and may now have regrettably passed away but for one and all I hope they enjoyed their shooting days on the Hamerton Estate.

My greatest thanks go to the beaters who informed me much more often where I went wrong than I informed them where they went wrong.

The wit of the beating side was inexhaustible. There was the beater who gave out a great 'hooray' when a gentleman shot a pheasant on the first day of a new season and when another beater asked: 'What the hell are you cheering for?' his reply came in a flash.

'He deserves a cheer. I watched him all though last season and he never hit a bloody thing.'

Then there was George Drage, a friend of long standing, who every time he came for a day's beating would say: 'Ought to have had my old gun with me this morning, Albert. There were a number of old cock pheasants on the roadside as I came along.'

And Stan Robins who, when a beater remarked about how he had observed a gentleman shooting at a low bird and he thought this was dangerous said in reply: 'You need not worry too much about that because he was shooting so low that if he hit you, you wouldn't get a pellet above your ankles.'

I could say a lot about these old friends but a lot of their remarks were unprintable!

My grateful thanks to the members of the family of the late Honourable Dorothy Bell and Major Bertram Bell who gave me their blessing when I suggested I write about the Hamerton Estate.

The cycle is just about complete. In 1955 Major Bell's letter to me asking if I would take on the post of gamekeeper for him at Hamerton said I wish you would take it on. The game stocks are so low and I would like to see them improve. Now, unfortunately, we are back to an even lower stock than there was then.

Basically there is no longer a Hamerton Estate, it is now just the Parish of Hamerton.

POSTSCRIPT

All in all I've had a good life. You could say that gamekeeping has been my life but that would not have been possible without the many interesting people I met over the years.

There were those who understood the land and what had to be done to provide a fair number of game birds for a good season's shooting. But there were also those who seemed to presume that sufficient birds would always be available for the gun without anything at all being done to produce and keep them on the estate.

Hard work has always been my motto and, together with observation and perseverance, I like to think that I have provided plenty of good shooting days for many gentlemen, and ladies, who enjoyed their sport to the full.

The majority also enjoyed watching a good dog working in the field and it has been my privilege to breed and train many dozens during my lifetime. I specialised in labradors and springer spaniels and have, over the years, placed many with my friends and colleagues for them to treat as their own.

I have also had a fascination for working terriers and have always kept one or two to help me with my work on the Hamerton Estate.

Now that I am retired you might think that I would be taking it easy but I am as busy as ever. Once the countryside is in your veins, it is there for all time.